EVERLASTING
spirituality

A truthseeker's guide to liberation.

Acharya Shree Yogeesh

Siddha Sangh Publications

SIDDHA SANGH PUBLICATIONS
9985 E. Hwy 56, Windom, Texas 75492
info@siddhayatan.org

Copyright © 2023 by Acharya Shree Yogeesh
Compilation/Editing: Sadhvi Siddhali Shree, Sarah Pretorius, Emily Halverson
Cover Design: Sadhvi Anubhuti

www.siddhayatan.org
www.acharyashreeyogeesh.com

All rights reserved. No part of this book may be reproduced or transmitted in any form, without written permission from the publisher, except by a reviewer, who may quote brief passages in a review; nor may any part of this book be reproduced, stored in a retrievable system, or transmitted in any form or by any means electronic, mechanical, photocopying, recording, or other, without written permission of the publisher.

ISBN - 1-7334750-5-1
ISBN - 978-1-7334750-5-1

Printed in the United States of America.

Disclaimer: Please note that not all exercises, diet plans, or other suggestions, mentioned in this book are suitable for everyone. This book is not intended to replace the need for consultation with medical doctors and other professionals. Before changing any diet, exercise routine, or any other plans discussed in this book, seek appropriate professional medical advice to ensure it is acceptable for you. The author and publisher are not responsible for any problems arising from the use or misuse of the information, materials, demonstrations, or references provided in this book. Results are not guaranteed.

TABLE OF CONTENTS

Part I — What

CH 1 — The Importance of Spiritual Mentorship 3
CH 2 — Finding a True Spiritual Teacher 13
CH 3 — Spiritual People, Truth Seekers, and Yogis 29
CH 4 — The True Spiritual Student 39
CH 5 — The Attributes of a True Spiritual Student 45

Part II — Why

CH 6 — Differentiating between True & False Teachers   61
CH 7 — Leaving Religion for Spirituality 69
CH 8 — Jainism: Teaching Religion or Spirituality 77
CH 9 — Tirthankaras: The Extraordinary Masters 83
CH 10 — Monkhood and the Multiple Paths to Truth 101

Part III — How

CH 11 — Siddha and Godhood 113
CH 12 — The Nature of Soul 121
CH 13 — Waking Up & Enlightenment in Everyday Life   135
CH 14 — Role & Importance of Health in Spirituality 153
CH 15 — Non-Violence: The Path to Personal & World .. 163
Peace
CH 16 — Practices of a True Student 183
CH 17 — How to Not Get Affected by Negativity 201
CH 18 — Pushing Through Life's Storms 209
CH 19 — Family Backlash After Awakening 217
CH 20 — The Beginning of Your Renewed Spiritual 225
Journey

- Also by Acharya Shree Yogeesh -

Secrets of Enlightenment, Vol. I
Secrets of Enlightenment, Vol. II
Awaken! A Handbook for the Truth Seeker
Chakra Awakening: The Lost Techniques
Soulful Wisdom & Art
Soul Talks: New Beginnings
Soul Talks: Path of Purification
Soul Talks: Power of Intention
Fasting: A Path for Healing, Transformation & Liberation

WHAT

The True Spiritual Teacher and Student

PART I

Chapter 1 —

The Importance of Spiritual Mentorship

Many truth seekers want to know: why is spiritual mentorship so important? Why is it important to have someone to guide them along a spiritual path?

For a serious truth seeker, it is essential to have a spiritual mentor. Without the right guidance, they can go down the wrong path—and once you are on the wrong path, it is very difficult to get on the right path again. Staying on the true course is very difficult without a spiritual guide or mentorship. Someone who will always tell you what to do, which way to go, and what to follow. A true spiritual mentor will always help you follow the real path.

Another benefit of spiritual mentorship is that the mentor will know whether the student is real or not. So in a way, the question is not if the spiritual teacher is real or not. The first question is...*Is the student real or not*? Most people don't think about it that way.

So, the question goes both ways. The teacher must be real, and the student must be real. It can be both, and if the student is real they will be able to tell if the teacher is real within a few months.

It appears that there are many spiritual teachers, mentors and gurus in the world. In my opinion, there are very few that are real. It may be confusing for seekers because they are desperate for the truth and it's hard to distinguish who is the real one because they all say the same things.

In the rainy season, many frogs are born and there will be a lot of frogs. Once the rain disappears, so do the frogs. For me, spiritual mentorship is something eternal, not temporary like the season of frogs.

Fake teachers or fake spiritual guides will not last long. Sooner or later, seekers will find out that maybe they lack knowledge, or they hurt others, or their intentions are not pure. Popularity doesn't make a spiritual teacher real nor the amount of followers they have. Eventually, if the seeker continues to seek (and it is in their karma to find a real one), they will come into contact with a real spiritual mentor.

In the presence of a real teacher, the students will feel a change inside of them. They will feel real peace. I've seen this happen around a truly spiritual person. Some might feel chills and goosebumps as their body becomes tuned into that same mood and presence, and it is almost as if their body begins to absorb that real information automatically.

If a mentor's teachings are not impressive, or if they're not transforming the students' lives, or they hurt others, or their impure intentions are revealed, or something else goes wrong with the mentor, the students will realize that the mentor is not real at all. They may also find out by sitting with a highly spiritual person that they feel something special inside of them and realize the other mentor didn't create the same reaction.

Spiritual mentors cannot be temporary. They cannot get popular in one day. If so, they might claim they are spiritual mentors, but people will come to know that they are not real.

With social media and the thrill of trying to be an influencer, there is an ocean of people trying to be a spiritual teacher or mentor, give advice, claim to heal or channel, and much more. Social media is a blessing and a curse. It can lead you to a real spiritual master or mentor or it can lead you to a fake. Spiritual mentors are forever, they don't get popular in one day because of a viral video - their teachings have to last, make an impact, and it can take years for them to be discovered. A spiritual mentor's sole focus is helping others awaken, not trying to get popular or be the best - they are beyond those things - that's why they're not temporary.

A real spiritual guide will work with a student when they are a real student. Spiritual teachers are seeking the quality of the student not quantity. The qualities of a student means how humble are they, how ready are they, how much of a seeker are they? Mentors are not here to entertain the curious minds of people, they're looking for the few that are really determined to work on themselves, transform their lower qualities into higher qualities, and awaken their souls. If the student is real, then the spiritual guide will appear. But if a student is not ready, even if the spiritual mentor is real, they cannot be guided. The student has to be ready.

Some students might feel lost in their search for a mentor. And, maybe they might not even come across a spiritual mentor or master physically in their life. They shouldn't be discouraged, because enlightened ones are available throughout the universe. Through the seeker's deep meditation, they can connect with enlightened souls. They might not see them or hear them physically, but if and when the soul is ready, they will find and connect with them. There is a popular saying, "When the student is ready, the teacher will appear." A master will tell students, "Stop living in the dark. The fun of the outside world is an illusion. What are you doing? Don't waste your life. Explore your soul, not the world, that is where you will find the bliss you're seeking."

The universe is full of enlightened ones and spiritual teachers – the spiritual masters are always available – it lacks students. Students need to be ready.

STUDENT READINESS

I have helped many students along their spiritual journey, so I know who is ready and who is not. People want to know why someone might not be ready to be a real student. The answer lies in many factors.

First of all, karma always blocks a person. If karma is in the way, when a person wants to do something, they cannot do it because their karma is blocking them. It is like the sun is shining, and yet very thick and heavy clouds are blocking its rays. It's the same way. Karma blocks people. They want to do something for the moment, and the next moment they don't want to do it. So, it shows their present ability and that something is going on in that person's life. Somehow somebody or something is blocking them, and the blockage is real.

People misunderstand the concept of karma. Many people think that karma is one word with one meaning, but it is much broader. Karma includes your illusion, your hallucination, your ignorance, your anger, your ego, your negativities, as well as your hate and jealousy. Everything is included in karma; it is all contained in that one word.

So if a student's karma is blocking them, there will not be clarity. They will only be ready when the karma starts to dissolve. The master has to enter into their consciousness to make it a little clearer and lend more clarity to their awareness. If a student remains near the master—even if they're not ready, but they stick around—they have a chance that their soul can be motivated and karma will begin to burn away.

The people seem to be ready, but they're not prepared because their karma is blocking them. And the most challenging karma is *mohaniya* karma, which means attachment. There are people who are truly ready to do something, but attachment blocks them. Mohaniya is a very strong block, despite their desire to know and experience the truth and reality. Eventually *darshanavarniya* karma, a type of karma that blocks right vision totally, comes to the surface. A person can become blind to the truth, and even if they want to do something they cannot. One clear example of someone with strong darshanavarniya karma is a person who sees a fake spiritual teacher as real or a real spiritual teacher as fake. The karma blocks the truth. Unfortunately, until that particular karma is removed they will live in a blind way. Many categories of karma can block the student from being ready. Things are not always what they appear to be.

Sometimes clearing karma takes time, and there is a right time to it. If the karma ripens before the right time, it may not fully work or there are complications. Like a baby born before its time, may not be perfect, similarly a person who is not ready to be on the real path. And we call that right path *samyaktva*, which is to be on the right track. But even while earnestly seeking, darshanavarniya karma can block them. That's why it is important to not have any karma or collect karma at all, it blocks the soul from what it wants – freedom.

The mohaniya attachment karma is much more known than darshanavarniya vision-blocking karma. To share a little more, an example of darshanavarniya karma in a student can be explained in this story. If a teacher is delivering a lecture and the student's darshanavarniya is very strong, the student will fall asleep. One of the symptoms of darshanavarniya is that the student becomes deaf to spiritual lessons. That specific karma will not only block one from hearing and understanding the message, but it can cause them to ridicule everything the teacher says because they are not able to learn. The lesson will be wasted because the word will not enter their hearts.

When the word doesn't penetrate the heart, it doesn't transform their life. The master will try to penetrate their consciousness so that this darkness will start to dissolve and the student will begin to see themselves more clearly, but it begins within the student. Even though there may be millions of spiritual seekers out there who seek guidance, how can a master help any of them awaken if their karma prevents them from receiving it? As I said before, it is still possible, but they will not find the right path immediately.

COMMON STUDENT STUMBLING BLOCKS

Many people consider themselves spiritual people, but because of karma they are blocked from the real teachings and are trapped in the incorrect teachings of false teachers or their own tainted misinterpretations.

There are teachers who might claim that they can provide students with samadhi, which is the divine state, in only a few minutes. How, you ask? By offering them ayahuasca, or LSD, or any drugs that cause you to hallucinate. These substances create powerful illusions in your mind, but the teacher tells them that they have had a spiritual experience. And yet it has all been a hallucination. It doesn't truly help them. Any substance that a teacher offers—be it alcohol or cannabis, hashish or opium—only creates more illusion and pollutes the body. The body is the best instrument for the soul and the soul needs a pure body to move towards enlightenment. That's why I strongly advise people to stay away from those who claim to be teachers, and yet offer you these substances that create big illusions that will harm your life, your path, and your opportunity to grow spiritually.

The best thing to do is find a really pure teacher who is also anti all of these things. When a teacher is anti all of those substances, that teacher can help you at least. If a teacher promotes or supports using substances, drinks alcohol, and is not vegetarian, then it automatically shows that they don't even hold that higher level of consciousness not to hurt or harm one's own body or the bodies of animals. Charisma, or a nice personality, or a popular speaker may be attractive and seem aware because they use the right words, but it doesn't mean they are living correctly – they will collect bad karma in their thoughts, actions, and words.

There are teachers that are still eating animals. There are sects in Buddhism who eat meat. If they are not even vegetarian yet, how can their own consciousness explore spirituality or teach it? Their consciousness will be so low and impaired, and yet millions of people will get trapped into their kind of teachings because they too are eating meat, taking drugs, and drinking alcohol. And they don't see the problem. This is why it is easy for millions of people to get trapped by false teachers because they share the same behavior and so they believe they are like-minded people. They think, "It's ok, the teacher does it so I'll follow them."

We need in this world again special souls like Mahavira, or a person like Parshvanath, a person like Adinath. They were totally against these kinds of things. They would never harm, hurt, or kill any living thing. Nevermind eating animals, which was beyond the question, but they would not even harm them! So we need those kinds of people again, and they are lacking unfortunately. That's why it's easy to get trapped into what's not real. Reality is sometimes right in front of you, and still you cannot see. God can be knocking at your door, and you don't hear it.

This happened with many misguided students. Even one of Buddha's cousins, who was also a monk living with him, was jealous of him because he wanted to be the popular one. He even wanted to kill Buddha multiple times. It shows that even when around someone highly spiritual, one cannot learn. Sometimes people are so blind they cannot see the teacher right in front of them because of their karma.

People also can get so mesmerized by certain actions. For example, if a teacher is giving a lecture and they are constantly crying, people might think they are a very compassionate teacher. An example of this happened in the United States, and yet this teacher proved to be very false. There was a big scandal because the teacher was collecting millions of dollars while they cried, pretending to be compassionate. The people we so mesmerized, even Christian people, they couldn't see the reality. But soon or later the fraud collapsed. That which is not real will eventually collapse. The real truth always remains.

Truth is eternal and so is spiritual mentorship. If it is real, it will last. And that mentor's teachings will guide you even if you are unable to speak directly with the master. Real teachers can still lift students' consciousness by meditating, even if nobody comes to them. They could be sitting in the Himalayas, with nobody in sight, but they can still lift a seeker's consciousness. How, you ask? Because they are at an elevated spiritual level or have a very strong aura that radiates so far that they can affect people within a thousand-mile radius.

The real search, the real discovery, is when one finds spiritual mentorship. It will be your biggest blessing. If you meet a real teacher even once, your life is totally transformed.

If I talk about something, the talk will benefit a lot of people, even the people who are not ready yet. They might not be ready for another ten years, but it will still help them. Even if they hear only one word, the people who are reading will fully grasp it. Through recording my teachings in books, videos and podcasts, I see that people can learn from me forever. Even when I am physically not here, my words will be here, and they can give generation-to-generation guidance. And I think once the message is out there, many people will still receive the benefits from following it.

I am honored to share my words in this book, for your benefit and all spiritual seekers who are ready to blossom into their highest-self.

Chapter 2 —

Finding a True Spiritual Teacher

When people ask how and where one can find a spiritual mentor, I will share essential clues that can help them understand exactly where to find one.

It can be difficult for people to find a spiritual mentor because often a true spiritual master or mentor will not tell you that he or she is a spiritual master. But if you understand these religious-based clues, you might be able to discern this on your own.

HOW TO SEEK A MENTOR

Clue 1 – Shramanic Tradition
The first clue is based on the oldest religion on Earth—the shramanic tradition, more specifically, we will focus on the Jain religion, which is one of the branches of the shramanic tradition. Within Jainism, there is a path to become a monk or a nun. There

are almost 12,000 Jain monks and nuns in the world today. Among one thousand Jain monks or nuns, there is a possibility that one of them could be a real spiritual mentor, only one of them. This creates only twelve possibilities to find a spiritual mentor out of twelve thousand presently. This is a possibility, not a guarantee, but at least there is a possibility. These monks and nuns have renounced everything—their families, their possessions, their wealth. They have no attachments. Their life is entirely devoted to spiritual progress and others. That is the first clue.

Clue 2 – Buddhist Tradition

The second clue is associated with another religion similar to Jainism, which is Buddhism. Buddhism is also from the shramanic tradition. Buddhism has the same system of monks and nuns who also renounce all attachments to pursue spirituality. There are millions of Buddhist monks and nuns around the world, so among them there is a possibility that one is a spiritual mentor.

Clue 3 – Catholic Tradition

The third religion that is similar is Catholicism. In Catholicism, they have monks and nuns too. There may not be a million Catholic monks and nuns, but in the distant past there used to be more. Because monks and nuns are renounced, they have nothing else to do except make spiritual progress. They pray a lot, they meditate a lot, and they want to find themselves. So once in a while, like Saint Francis, a monk can be a master. It has happened throughout history. It can occur in the future too.

Clue 4 – Judaic Tradition

The fourth clue can be found within the religion of Judaism. They have Hasidic monks, and they are not many, but there is a possibility you may find a master.

Clue 5 – Hindu Tradition

The fifth clue is the religion of Hinduism, but unfortunately, they don't have monks or nuns. In Hinduism, they are not renounced, but they call themselves *swami*, which means "he who is at one with himself." Essentially, swamis are devoted religious teachers and there are millions of them worldwide. But even among the hundreds of thousands of swamis around the world, it is possible that you may find only one that can be a spiritual master.

Spiritual masters are rare. But once you meet the spiritual mentor or spiritual master, it will be your luckiest day. Why? Because your life is going to be transformed. Sometimes when the master, the real master, the spiritual mentor, just looks at you deeply, even for just a few seconds, it can change your life. Sometimes people misunderstand and think, "Oh, all they need to do is look at me." Maybe their eyes were open, or maybe their eyes went toward you, but that is not the look I'm talking about. The real look means he or she absorbs you.

When a master or a spiritual mentor truly absorbs a student, that student is no longer a student. That student is on the way to becoming a spiritual guide or spiritual mentor themselves.

They begin to sprout hidden possibilities, and all hidden possibilities will start to wake up. That person can not only progress on his or her path, but they will also transform the lives of many other people in the future.

HOW TO RECOGNIZE A MENTOR

If you were to Google "How do I find a spiritual mentor?", you will get a million different results, and it would be challenging to determine a real spiritual mentor from the unenlightened teachers. That's why I suggest you travel. I believe the best way to find a spiritual mentor is to travel to a monastery or an ashram. Then again, you may even meet them on an airplane, or train, or just walking around. Sometimes they are walking around in public, and you just don't see it.

Once, I was in Nepal with a group of students, and someone walked up and asked me for a blessing. They had recognized me from YouTube, and now I was walking around in their country. So it is true, the master can be anywhere. You just have to have sharp eyes, or I will say "discovering" eyes in order to discover them. Otherwise, they might one day be right in front of you, but you won't see them.

Buddha walked everywhere, and still, many people missed him. Mahavira was once out and about and even his future disciples missed him. A spiritual master is hard to see if a person is not ready. And if a person is not ready, they cannot see it. Sometimes you have a real diamond in your hands, but people think it is just an unimportant little stone if they don't know anything about diamonds. You have to know about it. You have to have feelings about it. You have to have some kind of realization about it. That is how you will recognize a master. When I was asked what's the percentage of truth seekers that come across a master, but they are unable to recognize him or her? I said that over 90% of people have come across a master, but they could not recognize the master. That's a considerable amount of people that don't have eyes to see. They need to have real eyes that truly see. They need to open their third eye, and then they can recognize the master. To open up your third eye, you must have clarity and the right vision.

It's good karma to encounter a real teacher, but it doesn't necessarily mean you will learn from them in this life. Good karma means you could have a little taste of it, and then it goes away. Like how the wind can suddenly crash into you–it touches you, but then it is gone and doesn't affect anything about your life after that moment.

To realize that one is a master, you must close your two eyes. You have to become like the blind. When you see through these naked eyes, your two natural eyes alone will not recognize the master. A master can only be identified when seen through the third eye.

The third eye must be activated at some point in the presence of the master. It can be started by itself, even by chance, or by mistake. Maybe wished for by a master, and through that it was activated. Readiness is the most important thing.

When I first meet a soul, I smile and look at them. Sometimes I say, "What are you doing here?" Or "What are you doing in this world? Just come, and have a cup of tea." When I say that, they either get it or don't. It is up to them, but I try to wake them up. On a soul level, I just try to blow a big wind, a big storm. A storm of detachment, a storm of love, a storm of compassion. In this kind of storm, when I blow a little bit towards them, they begin to feel it and they even may spend time with me this life, but they will be affected on the soul level.

YOUR FIRST ENCOUNTER

The first thing a master will do when they take on a real student is "crush their head" or "chop their head off." Not literally, of course. I just mean they bring them from their head down to their heart. The heart is where the spiritual journey begins.

A master's duty is not to make a student, but to make a student a master. That's what a master's duty is, to be like a candle. When one candle is lit, it can then light another candle. That is the master's duty, one at a time. The master who is trying to make a big crowd with many students is not a master at all. But rather, he or she makes a student a master on an individual basis. That's what masters will do for their students.

Genuine truth seekers, or real students, must use the clues I have given and dig out the answer for themselves. If they choose to not use these clues, they will be roaming around among the fake masters and are never going to be awakened or begin their journey in this life.

They might momentarily feel something because this person is unusual, or totally different from others they have met. But after a few months, they will find out that the master is not real. Reality is manifested when after learning from the master your life begins to transform quickly, within sometimes only an hour. Within a few days, you are different. You will transform your life totally.

It is up to the seeker how they are going to find them. They have to search. Is it technology? These days technology plays a significant role. They can hear a true mentor's teachings even if they are far away. They can still feel it. There is a way to find it, just close your eyes and just think about it.

In essence, an authentic spiritual mentor will simply teach you something. They might only share a little bit, but you will have your self-discovery. A spiritual mentor ignites a journey of self-discovery; the path is yours to walk.

BENEFITS OF STUDYING UNDER A MASTER

How important is it to be a student or a disciple of an enlightened one?
There are a few reasons.

The first reason is that when you learn from an enlightened person, you learn directly from the source. If you learn from other teachers, they may have received their information from books written by common people and not enlightened ones. People generally may know a lot of information because their minds have been programmed since childhood. Since the time we're babies, we've been fed information from the outside world. If you learn from someone who is not an enlightened one, however, you receive second-hand information. You are learning from people who learn from books. You want to learn from someone who is directly connected to the direct source of information. The only direct source of knowledge is the soul.

A person becomes enlightened when their soul is fully awakened. At that time, the knowledge begins to overflow. The enlightened one can help students wake up. It's like a shortcut to liberation. The ultimate goal is to be liberated. Liberated from suffering, pain, ignorance, illusion, hallucination, the pain of negativity, anger, and emotions. These are what make a person's life miserable.

Psychology and self-help books can share a lot of information, but they will not necessarily help you find the right path. To be an enlightened person's student means you are seeking the right path. Once you are on the right path, on the right track, you will arrive where you want to go. So, the first reason is the importance of receiving guidance directly from the source.

Secondly, if you learn now from the enlightened one, you will have less chances of being led astray. You will always go in the right direction because, as I mentioned several times, when you live with or are close to the enlightened master, although it's not easy, the master will correct you along the way. It can be very difficult because an enlightened one will see where you're making mistakes, and they will always make you aware. The student may be annoyed, irritated, or frustrated, even hurt but they will always learn.

Another reason an enlightened master is needed is because, as aforementioned, the master doesn't want to make you a student at all. He or she wants you to become a real student—and this only happens if that student becomes a teacher. Unless you become a teacher and master, you cannot become a student. Before that, you are just an illusion. You are not the right person to learn.

It's tough to find an enlightened one who will tell you the truth. The truth is not always easy to digest, and so their students are few. In contrast, other so-called enlightened masters want to show you the crowd. They will tell you that they have a million students, and they want to put on a show. But those are not real students, because none of them have the potential to become masters. Real students see through a fake teacher or so-called enlightened master.

Real students are very rare. Sometimes we call a student a disciple, and disciple-hood is not easy. You have to surrender everything to the teachings of the master. You have to let go of your ego and your anger. But other people will misguide you. They will tell you that you have to surrender your money. They call it in the Indian language *tan man dhan*. *Tan* means your body, *man* means your mind, and *dhan* means your wealth. That's why people become stuck in illusion - money has nothing to do with surrendering.

ASSESSING READINESS FOR THE FIRST STEPS

Among the different steps that a student must take to begin this journey, it is vital to meet the enlightened one in person. Even if they are listening to my podcast or watching my YouTube channel, the personal energy is missing, the experience through the senses are missing, like the vision and eye contact is missing. It is like the aliveness is missing. When they meet me face-to-face, they don't miss those things. Aliveness will be there, and they can feel it immediately.

Many people are sensitive to what they begin to feel through listening to my videos and are deeply immersed in the subjects I am talking about. They will start to feel connected to the deepest part of their being. It is amazing when you watch an enlightened person. You can not take your eyes away from them as you become fully immersed in the depth of their being. Actually, two reactions can happen. Either they go into a trance and fully surrender their ego, anger, or emotions. (Not surrender like people think or surrender physically. No, that is not the question. If surrendering is what is bothering you, if anger bothers you, surrender your anger. If your ego bothers you, surrender your ego. If any other emotion or negativity bothers you, surrender it, then be pure.) A student either goes right away into this surrendering state of consciousness, or they will simply feel a lot of calmness and patience in their being. And the second thing that can happen is they can turn off the videos, because it doesn't click for them. The master is seeking students who have the potential to be a master, anyways.

The master has a particular way of teaching students. They don't want a student, they want a master, so they need to see that the student can progress, that they have potential. If the master doesn't see the ability, the person might get turned off, and they will go away. They might wake up later. Either of these reactions are positive things.

But there is an exception, that can also happen two separate ways. There is a chance that the master may suddenly put all things out in the open, which are hidden inside of you. When these truths come to the surface and they cannot take them, they will run away or be humbled and remain. It is possible that a person will be allergic for a while, then get involved again.

Enlightened masters are selective about the students and disciples that they accept. You would think that masters would want all the students, all of the disciples so that they can help them. But there's a different side to it. The students can have an adverse reaction. They may not even be interested in learning from the master. For some people, it is not their karma or their ego that blocks them from recognizing the master. It is simply not the right time for them. They need to live through many cycles of birth, life, and death before they are ready to recognize and work with a master. If it happens, if some people come back, they begin to put effort and realize.

TAKING THE FIRST STEPS, RIGHT WHERE YOU ARE

Students all over the world reach out and express that they want to make more of a commitment to be my student. If they want to elevate their spiritual journey, I share with them these initial seven steps they can follow, which will help them along the right path.

Of the seven steps I always teach, the first step is non-violence. Non-violence is not to kill and not to hurt any living being. Eating vegetarian is included in non-violence. If they are a meat eater and stop eating today, it will take six years to cleanse the whole body and they must begin this process immediately. That is the first step they have to take.

Suppose they are still eating meat, eggs are actually meat. But people need to learn what meat is. Meat is anything that moves, from bugs to cows. Anything born with organs through the female reproductive organs is considered meat. Even though eggs are also considered meat, Gandhi taught that because eggs do not have babies in them, they are vegetarian. It is a misleading teaching. I understand what he was trying to say but still eggs are a form of flesh and cannot be considered vegetarian because they come through the female reproductive organ. So that is the first step out of seven.

To be enlightened, one must be vegetarian and not eat eggs - there is no exception - for karmic reasons.

Second, I always emphasize that they never lie. A big lie, at least.

Small lies, mother, father, everybody does it. But a big lie can hurt somebody's life, kill them, and they can commit suicide because you tell a big lie about them, and it turn it shames them and they cannot handle it so they take their own life. For example, if someone tells a big lie about someone else, spreads a big rumor, and that person cannot mentally take it, they might consider suicide. That person's suicide is the liar's karma. Big lies collect a lot of karma, so stay away from big lies.

The third step is non-stealing. If something doesn't belong to you, don't take it. If you find somebody's information, or if you have sensitive information about them, you've got to inform them. Non-stealing includes not stealing or robbing from people. Like business people, a lot of big businesses steal a lot.

The fourth principle they can follow is no hunting–not hunting any birds, any animal, nothing. No insects. Even if fishing is your hobby, those on the spiritual path will avoid doing it anymore because fish are harmed by this action. They get stuck into that little hook and it hurts. Even killing a simple lizard that is also hunting. Hunting hurts and kills, put yourself in their place, how would you feel if you were hunted?

The fifth thing that's important to follow is no sexual misconduct. If you are married, be loyal to your partner, or if you are not married and you have a partner, you must still be loyal to them. If you are single, don't be promiscuous. In love, energy is not lost but rather gained. When you are with people out of physical desire/lust and there is no love, energy is lost. This also includes not going to prostitutes, strip clubs and not watching or engaging in pornography.

The sixth step you can take is not to gamble. You can lose a lot of your money when you gamble, and it is not a good idea to engage in this practice. With gambling, so much karma is collected from lying, feeling guilty and being deceitful.

The seventh step is one that you must follow to stay on the right path–and that is abstaining from alcohol, drugs, and tobacco. Whatever they are smoking, or any prescription medicine or substance they are addicted to–they must begin now. It might take 12 years to overcome. What will you do? Generally speaking, it takes six years to fully remove these habits and toxins from your being, so you can make faster progress by releasing them right away. There is no freedom in addiction. Addiction isn't spiritual, there is no freedom in it. It shows the substances control you.

Many new-age spiritual people and practitioners turn to marijuana, LSD, mushrooms, and things like ayahuasca because they say it's natural and that it's okay because God created it. Not every plant on earth needs to be used. If a person truly wants to be a student of mine, they have to be willing to practice this last vow and not use any of these things. Those substances will make them stray from the real path and they will not remain on it.

It is better not to have those things in your life. It is all included. Stay away from things like marijuana, it's an herb, but it can become addictive. I know thousands of people who have lost their jobs because they became lazy. They begin to only desire to be in that moment smoking marijuana and they become sluggish and slothful, and can even lose their jobs because they no longer want to go into work, preferring to live in that mode under the influence. It is a very addictive herb.

It can be used sparingly if somebody has arthritis, but not through smoking it. Instead, you can put one leaf into a glass bottle of water and leave it in the sun for one week. That then becomes an effective medicine for arthritis. You then take about two tablespoons of that water every day. It will help remove the pain without the need to smoke it. This herb can even begin to heal little cancer cells, but not by inhaling it via smoking. As I said before, smoking cannabis will cause you to become addicted, and that's why I include it in this step with this warning–stay away from addiction. Shunning these things will protect you from addiction and give you a better chance to grow spiritually. For medicinal purposes, there is a little flexibility.

If you follow these steps before encountering an enlightened master, you will come closer to being a student and have a better chance when you meet them for your energy to be awakened. If you don't take any steps along the path and just want to meet a master out of excitement, the excitement will fade. Students have to be real and ready and willing to follow all of the steps.

DEDICATED VOWS

Is there a particular vow people take? Yes, I recite the vow to them, and they must repeat after me these spiritual words, in Sanskrit, which is how they confirm their committed adherence. If they break this vow, they will ruin their lives, and they cannot blame me. My responsibility is not theirs, and theirs is not mine. Don't take the vow if you intend to break it. If you take it, don't break it.

Many students believe they are ready and want to be on the path, but still have other responsibilities. I don't blame them. Even if they learn a little bit, I still consider them as beginning on that path. I meet them where they are.

I have students worldwide that I try to visit when I travel. One student continued to reach out to me from Singapore, and he was very, very persistent about being in touch with me and receiving my blessings. Recently, by chance, I traveled to Singapore and he visited me for fifteen or twenty minutes, which he reported to have changed his life.

So you never know if it could be you. Be in touch, be ready, and seriously consider becoming more committed as a student. If you're ready to take these seven vows from me, get in touch.

Chapter 3 —

Spiritual People, Truth Seekers & Yogis in Modern Spirituality

In the world of modern spirituality, there are a lot of different names for spiritual people. For example, we hear the term spiritual practitioner, or people say they are truth seekers. Some people say they are yogis, but what word best describes the genuinely spiritual person?

Here are my thoughts on labels and what words make the most sense. There is a story of an Arab man who had two wives. His first wife comes, she asks, "Who is the prettiest woman in the world?" The husband replies, "Of course, you are the most beautiful person." His second wife then comes and asks the same question. The husband replies, "But of course you are." Then when he is not at home, the two wives talk. "He says I am the most beautiful." "No, he said I am the most beautiful." The wives decide that they will ask their husband this question together. That evening when the three of them are together, the wives ask their husband who he thinks is the most beautiful person on earth. Now he is stuck in a difficult situation, no? So he managed by saying, "You are more beautiful than each other."

So you see, people always find a way to stake their claim on which words they believe are best. Some say yogis are the most incredible, and some say, "Oh, spiritual people are the most incredible." Some say, "No truth seekers are the most incredible." All of these titles are just ideas. And you know where this idea starts? In the United States. In the U.S., they don't produce the product, but they sell the idea. They are experts in selling profitable ideologies.

On the other hand, genuine truth seekers appear very peaceful, so serene, and down to the earth. But then unfortunately they begin to sell that idea too. Suddenly spiritual people are marketed as the friendliest people on earth. They are always sitting quietly, peacefully, and in meditation. These ideas are crafted beautifully, and a beautiful notion sells–and the U.S. knows how to market anything. Any idea can be sold if someone knows how to market it.

I remember a long time ago when I was living in India reading an incredible book that, strangely, nobody seemed to want to buy. The author came to me and shared how worthwhile their book was, but nobody was purchasing it. I told the author to simply change the title. "For the book to sell, the title has to be attractive. For the average buyer, who cares what is inside?" The author understood this idea was worth trying. I suggested to him maybe four different names, and soon after he changed the title. The book began to sell like hotcakes.

So these ideas of being a *yogi*, or a *truth seeker*, or *being spiritual* are all just ideas, labels. In Western countries, they know how to sell these labels.

They are all incredible people if they are real yogis, who are interested in going deep into the samadhi state. Yoga is just *yogashchittvrittirnirodhah* where all these ideas stop, and the yoga, or union, begins. But where there are the mind waves and mind ripples still playing on your life, that is not a yogi. A yogi is beyond that. When he or she is into it, they're connected to the soul. I can guarantee those who are connected to the soul are connected to all living beings. And the most problematic and hardest thing in the world is to be connected to yourself. But once you connect to yourself, everything is connected to you. Like when people say that we are all children of God, that means we are connected to God. Children are not apart from God. But can we feel that? If so, then you become a yogi.

Truth seekers are incredible people too. Why? They are incredible in the sense that they are seeking the truth. They don't want to be in illusion, in ignorance, bound by some kind of idea that doesn't work. So they try to seek the truth. Where do they search for the truth? Not outside. They want to go deep into their consciousness, and that is where they find it. Truth is hidden there.

Many people consider themselves very spiritual. I often hear stories of how someone experiences a little incident in their life and voila they think, "Oh, I am spiritual. I am a healer. I'm a master." They say, "My kundalini has risen." "My kundalini has awakened." From a little experience to grand statements, it shows ego - not spirituality.

I have heard many stories from new-age people in the United States who say that as they smoke pot or do ayahuasca, their kundalini begins to rise. That is not kundalini. That is whatever is hidden inside of you beginning to come up on the surface. Maybe a lot of things were hidden inside of you, and you didn't know how much there was. Through the chemicals, this hidden energy came to the surface, like a person under the influence of alcohol. You get drunk and you begin to talk. Many people when they are drunk, as I've heard and you've seen, they talk a lot. It doesn't mean they are spiritual if they are talking and saying something interesting or poignant. It is an illusion, artificially induced.

But reaching spirituality in the United States can often resort to these means unfortunately. Gurus imagine their own heaven. They create their own Bali or Amazon jungle and false shamanism that offers them drugs or drinks. Do they even know where shamanism comes from? It is a shamanic tradition. *Samanas* is another name for shamans, those who put all their efforts into opening up the soul. But not with the drink, smoking pot, or sitting around sweat lodges. No. Sitting with *you and yourself* will create miracles in your life. Instead, their followers take what's offered them and get lost in the drink or substances, but in the end they remain the same people. The modern shamans today are much different from the original samanas.

DANGERS OF "BECOMING SPIRITUAL"

It's perilous to be a yogi or to be a truth seeker, or to be a spiritual person. Why? Because I have found that it can create a lot of egos. People think they've arrived once they call themselves a yogi or spiritual person. They've discovered the truth. They begin to think, "I found it. I found it. I know it, I know it." Truth cannot be found in one day, and spirituality cannot be developed in one moment. It is a long search. Their ego stops them just as soon as they start.

Their situation is like a mouse who found a little piece of turmeric. Turmeric is an herb like ginger, the root. It has medicinal properties. The other mice come to him with their health and pain problems, and the mouse with the turmeric tells them that he has medicine for them. He gives each a little piece of turmeric. "I know how to heal you. Eat this, and your pain will disappear." And this little mouse now has a big ego. He says, "I am an herbal doctor." He starts to think he is a doctor who can remove any and all pain just because he found one little piece of turmeric root.

That is what it is like for all these yogis who have egos, I call them so-called yogis, and so-called truth seekers, and so-called spiritual people because they are full of ego. They are self-entitled, and these word titles themselves begin to create ego. I am a yogi. I am a truth seeker.

But there are small numbers of people who are not into that ego and are real yogis. The ego doesn't touch them. They can be a truth seeker, they can be spiritual people. The ego doesn't touch them. They dissolve the ego. When they dissolve their ego, there is no difference between a yogi, a truth seeker, or a spiritual person. They are all the same. When you are egoless, you arrive at the same destination. The ego is what makes you separate. The biggest enemy of humans is the ego. We call ego *ahamkara*. Ahamkara is the greatest illusion in a human's life.

It can be difficult for people to overcome their egos. They may honestly say, "I teach yoga. Therefore, I am a yogi." Or they'll call themselves a spiritual teacher just because they teach a meditation workshop. But how do you help them come down to earth to see reality? And that reality is that what they are declaring is their ego, their persona, but not necessarily their genuinely developed spirituality.

People operating in the ego will feel hurt if they think you are calling them out. But the irony is that they are not a real yogi or a true spiritual teacher in the first place if you *have to* tell them.

In the end, you can either try and help wake people up or allow them to learn independently. Most people will come to the point they will realize they are wrong. With many people, I have to hit them and kick them (metaphorically, of course) with ideas before they come to the realization. Their ego distracts them in the wrong direction, so I try to distract them in the right direction and bring them some awareness so they can see and then forget the ego.

If someone is distracted by silver, if they have achieved silver along their spiritual journey, then I will show them gold. Then they will be distracted by the gold automatically. I will show them better things; thus, their ego will be distracted. Once they are distracted by the ego, you must show them a better path. This is how I can support truth seekers ready to embody that term fully.

Sometimes, I use other methods to help people dissolve their egos. The teaching style depends on the person and how that person will learn best. It's not something I decide beforehand. It's not a prefixed idea to distract them with gold or diamonds. I have to see when the person is in front of me, that's what all these masters will do as soon as the student comes. They know how to shut their ego down or make them humble themselves and come down to earth, but a person has to be in front of the master. If they are not, it can be challenging. It is difficult just to give a general or blanket statement about how I can help someone dissolve their ego because every soul is different. Everybody's karma is different.

Only an absolute master or advanced spiritual person can help you in this way. The concept of "selling ideas" is interesting because, here in the U.S. or Europe, going to Bali for spirituality or yoga has become a great selling tool as a way to somehow magically dissolve ego or achieve enlightenment. The romantic idea of going to India, and that India is the only spiritual country where these changes can occur, is definitely leveraged in the marketing of spiritual and yoga retreats. I always say, just close your eyes, you're already there. That doesn't even require a plane ticket.

This can be very helpful for a lot of people to hear because people can easily get caught up in labels and stuck in boxes regarding how spirituality should be. It's ironic that many people are trying to escape religion because it has created too many boxes for them. Then they want to be spiritual because they don't want to be confined by religion anymore. But then they get stuck in more categories and boxes again, only with different names. If they find an authentic spiritual master and receive the proper guidance, they'll be able to get out of all categories, remove all labels, and free their soul. They need a lot of guidance, which can only happen when they are present or ready to hear it.

"SPIRITUALITY LITE" VS TRUE SPIRITUALITY

Have you ever heard the saying that the most challenging thing as a spiritual student is to live with their master? When you don't live with a master, they cannot see when the student makes a mistake. But when you live with a master or spend time with them, they will always see and point out your mistakes to help you grow. They will be able to see in their student's eyes and know already where to start to do the hard work of hammering the ego in order to peel off the layers of karma—and people don't want to do the hard things. They want the light version of spirituality, "spirituality lite."

It is not easy to live with the master. Still, if you're a seeker, if you're a spiritual person, if you're a real yogi, then you will be willing to put yourself into the presence of a master so that you can wake up and go through the experience of whatever you need to go through to become enlightened - whether in this life or in a future life. It's not easy to wake up. It's not easy for your buttons to be pushed—and a master does so, of course, with the intention to push you out of the dark and into the light. It is said that watching or listening is effortless, but you learn less. Yes, you get seeds through listening, but some seeds take a long time to germinate and the conditions have to be just right. But if you spend time with the master, like a plant in a greenhouse, growth can happen with care and steadiness.

My chief disciple, Sadhvi Siddhali Shree, considers herself "a work in progress" who has come a long way. She shared how grateful she is that I have helped point out the things to her that she could not see because of her karma or lack of awareness.

She has studied under me for nearly twenty years; and if you had first met her then, you would see that she was completely different. She recognizes that even though she was a very spiritual person, a real truth seeker, she had a huge spiritual ego at the time. She thought she knew everything, and then under my guidance, she realized she knew nothing, and that's the right place you want to be in. You want to be in a place where you know you don't know anything because that keeps you humble. That is the path to enlightenment. That's when you can truly embody the definition of a "spiritual person," a genuine truth seeker. When you're humble you can learn.

Chapter 4 —

The True Spiritual Student

In the first chapter, we talked about the importance of a genuine spiritual mentor. So now the question is, *who is the real spiritual student*?

There are millions of people all around the world that say that they are spiritual, but does that mean they are all real students? For me, the answer is no. It's a matter of whether you're talking about quantity or quality. Real students are like quality. There is an abundance of people who wish to be spiritual students. There are millions of them. However, real students are challenging to find. There are not many of them in this world.

If you see a big crowd of people, like a yoga festival, the people might seem very spiritually minded. It's easy for people to get mesmerized by the crowd and think they are very spiritual. They're peaceful, talk very softly, and seem very nice. They look like they are enjoying themselves, but they don't know much about what it means to be spiritual. They are not real students. Why? It's because they still love their things. They have too many attachments to material things. They are still smoking marijuana and may still be taking drugs and eating animals or using animal products. You can see how it can be tough to find real students.

No, these people are not even close to being real students yet. When a student is ready, they drop everything. And this process happens suddenly because their heart finally gets it. Their heart just gets pierced by the truth. One word of truth can pierce the students' hearts, and when it does, they are ready to walk on the right path.

When a student is ready and their heart has been pierced by truth, this kind of pain that feels like joy or happiness enters the heart. Sometimes this feeling can bring tears to their eyes. I have seen students with tears, and people think they are overwhelmed with devotion. That's not entirely the case. These tears fall because something so profound, so true has clicked for them. Like a spark of light in their soul has been lit. This clicking can happen for a genuine student at any time.

DEVOTION

The first test to know if a student is real is whether or not they are fully devoted. Are they devoted? The heart of a real student is filled with devotion and dedication. It's important to know that devotion only happens in two ways, devotion to God or devotion to the teacher, their spiritual mentor.

You first see if their heart is filled up with this devotion. The real student has surrendered to whatever the master says they must do. If the master says it is night, even if it is daytime, the student will say yes, it is true. That's the level of dedication they embody. The journey of devotion doesn't begin in a person's mind but it starts in their heart. That's where their spiritual journey begins. It's a surrender of their heart, and most people have a difficult time with this because of their ego.

Once they embody devotion, we say that people are on the samyak path. *Samyak* means the right path. In Sanskrit, there are many words for students, including; Shishya, Bhakta, and Chela, and for females, Cheli. *Shishya* means "one who now wants to learn a lot, one who wants to learn how to uplift his or her soul." There is also a word for those getting even closer to this level of devotion and learning. We call them *shravak* and *shravika*. Shravak means someone who is a good listener; when they listen, they listen with their heart. And when it goes into their heart, it creates so much joy, happiness, and peace that they want to learn even more.

These students are challenging to find. They can be anyone. They can be ordinary people (shravak or shravika) or they can be monks and nuns. Monks and nuns are more serious because they have more time to learn because they renounced the world. Because shravak and shravika are householders, they have to raise their children and have a lot of other responsibilities.

Once this Shishyatva is ready for the right path, the master will appear before them. These real students are prepared to follow the spiritual master and walk on the path, regardless of their life. It doesn't matter what lifestyle they come from or if they are monks, anyone can become a real student.

An example of full devotion can be found in the story of a woman named Meera who was a student who lived in India nearly 500 years ago. Meera was so devoted to God that her heart overflowed with it, and every time she sat down, she would write a devotional song. Still to this day, her music is broadcasted on India First, a radio station that used to be called Broadcast India. They play Meera's songs on the radio and TV first thing in the morning because that's how they want to start their day, with devotion. This is just one reason why India seems like such a spiritual country, but that doesn't necessarily mean you only find real students there. Real students can be anywhere. Real students are everywhere.

While some might think that love is the same as devotion, they are not the same things. Love has nothing to do with devotion or compassion. Some people might say, "Oh, we are very loving and compassionate towards animals," and they think because of this that they are very spiritual. Certainly to be loving and compassionate towards animals is an outstanding quality, but it has nothing to do with devotion. Devotion is when you totally dissolve your thoughts, mind, and sense of self.

That said, if real students have love, it can increase their devotion, so it is a beginning step. Those who are filled up with love, can receive great happiness and relaxation when they are connected with all of nature. When they go to the forest or the ocean, when they see the moon, and the stars, they feel connected to the oneness of everything. That is also a symptom of the real students.

EGOLESSNESS

The second test to know if a student is real and fully devoted is egolessness. True learning cannot happen if you have a big ego. Ego is often the main problem, and the ego resides in your head. Therefore, your head has to be metaphorically and thoroughly chopped off, and a real master will be the one to do it. Not literally, of course! It just means that your ego has to go, and when your ego is gone completely then you can fully surrender. Egolessness is another test of a real student. That is when spiritual awakening can happen, and with a master it can happen quickly.

A guru is like a clay pottery maker, who puts a pot in the sun to dry after they have formed the pot with their hands. However when the pot was in the sun, it cracked a bit, so the pottery maker put one hand inside the pot while the other patted down the outside in order to fill in the cracks.

The guru is like the pottery maker, and the real student is like the pot with cracks that the guru helps to fill. The real student may have a lot of shortcomings and weaknesses, and so the teacher has to build them up and smooth them out. The spiritual teacher will have one hand symbolically inside the student while the other hand steadies the outside while filling up the cracks so that the pot can stand the pressure and won't fall apart.

The real student trusts the teacher, and even when spiritual upliftment is challenging, the teacher protects them. The real student doesn't run away when it gets hard. Even if the teacher were to scream and yell, the real student knows of their compassion and their intention is to protect them. The immature student will run away as soon as it becomes too much because they are not entirely devoted and their ego cannot take it.

In the following chapter, we will go deeper into this subject of becoming a real student and the personal attributes one must possess. There is so much more to learn!

Chapter 5 —

The Attributes of a True Spiritual Student

In the last chapter, I shared that one essential quality of a "real student" is that they will be detached from the world. In this chapter, we'll go even deeper into the behaviors that happen once this non-attachment occurs. This is what makes a real student stand out and differentiates them from others who may believe they are ready for the spiritual path but are not quite there yet.

If the greatest sign of a real student must possess a pure heart, then what does this mean? It means they have a heart full of love, compassion, devotion, and, most of all, purity. It is one of those symptoms that when a genuine student possesses it, you can identify it very clearly. Purity isn't a virtue that arises out of nowhere. Purity has to have innocence as a foundation upholding it.

I want to be clear that the innocence I am talking about here has nothing to do with the sexual connotations people commonly associate with it. This type of innocence also doesn't mean ignorance. It doesn't mean ignoring the truth or the realities around you. To embody innocence is to possess that child-like state of wonder, and awe, a heart of pure goodness and love. A child's innocence means they view the world with optimism and the unpolluted belief that people are ultimately good. They are innocent because they have not been corrupted by ego and lower qualities like greed, resentment, prejudice, and judgment. Truly innocent people are scarce these days and are hard to find.

Innocence is also unshaken by emotions because emotions go up and down, like ripples or high tides. To react to emotions is a sign of an impure heart, a symbol of the ego, and an impure heart cannot cope with reality. Overlooking innocence, many people think that a real student has to have a lot of knowledge, but that's not true. To have a pure heart doesn't require that, just like a baby doesn't have any knowledge yet. What a baby fears or experiences is in the present moment. When a baby smiles or cries, it experiences these emotions without holding on to them. This has nothing to do with knowledge.

PURITY AND KNOWLEDGE

That said, knowledge is good in many ways. It heightens your intellectual level and can mean you are intelligent. It means your instrument of the mind is very developed and that you can grasp the knowledge very quickly and easily. Those are all positive things. But it is also important to remember that being very intelligent doesn't necessarily mean that you are on a spiritual path or that you are prepared to be a real student.

You hear how many scientists, whom society considers some of the world's most knowledgeable and intellectual people, are becoming more and more atheist. Their rational, logical brain deters them from spirituality. Therefore, knowledge does not necessarily make someone a real student. To recognize your ignorance is better than to boast of your intelligence. The person who says, "I know nothing" is like a blank slate. An entirely blank slate is ready to receive. There is room for the teacher to write on his or her heart.

This student will progress quickly because they will not block their learning with comparisons. Sometimes when a person has a lot of knowledge, there is a lot of noise in their mind. They will always compare what the teacher tells them with what they think they already know. Sometimes knowledge alone, when not paired with humility and openness, can create a lot of trouble. In that sense, you can see how knowledge doesn't lend itself to spirituality. If you begin to compare, then you're never going to learn. You will become stuck in your mind. Real students do not live in their heads; they live in their purified hearts. They also have a pure vision and are not polluted.

Who is polluted, you may ask? I can give you the symptoms.

Digambar is a Jain sect that used to have an Acharya (spiritual leader) named Kundakunda Acharya. *Kunda* means "not intelligent at all." So the irony is that his name is Kundakunda, but the Digambar believe he was the most intellectual person on Earth.

He wrote in one of his books, "*Dansan bhattha bhattha. Dansan bhatthassa nathi nivarnam. Sijjhanti chariya bhattha. Dansan bhattha na sijjhanti."* This translates to, "He who is polluted, whose heart is polluted, has no vision." This vision does mean what you see with your eyes, but your right vision is your ability to grasp the right path. It also means that when your vision is not polluted, your knowledge is not polluted and you can truly see. If you depend on what other people tell you, your vision and knowledge are polluted.

PURITY AND RIGHT VISION

Real students must have the right vision. Kundakunda said that this is a possibility, that *chariya bhattha sijjhanti*, which means that the person polluted by character or conduct can still change and improve their conduct and behavior. It's possible that this person can be *sijjhanti*, which means they can cross the ocean of suffering. Although it is possible, *Dansan bhattha na sijjhanti*, which means someone who is polluted in vision, is never liberated.

Having the right vision is very important for a real student. If they don't have the right vision, they don't know where to go. They can be deceived by fake teachers because they don't have their own right vision. They may be full of knowledge, but their right vision is lacking.

Therefore having the right vision must be the first symptom of a real student, even before knowledge. Right vision can take you out of pollution so that your heart may become truly pure. An actual student becomes innocent with the right vision. And real purity can enter their heart when their vision is right. Even without knowing anything, not having read any books or collected billions of facts and information, that person can be liberated and follow the spiritual path.

This has happened in the past, it occurs in the present, and it will happen in the future too. Let me give you an example. Once a man told his spiritual teacher that he was ready to become a monk and wished to do so. He said, "I am ready to renounce everything. I'm ready to burn my house. I am ready to detach."

The teacher initiated him, and this man became a monk. Then the teacher tried to give him his first lesson. The teacher would teach him in the morning, but by the evening, the man had forgotten everything from the lesson. The teacher tried to teach him more discipline, but still, the man forgot everything. The teacher tried to teach the man for six months, then a year, but still this man continued to forget everything even though he was putting in great effort.

Finally, feeling frustrated, the man asked the teacher to give him a technique so that his soul could, at last, be liberated. The teacher recognized he was a real student, a genuine truth seeker, but because the man could not memorize his lessons he didn't feel confident on how to liberate his soul.

The teacher decided on a simple technique. "Why don't you start sweeping this place? Do you see this broom? It doesn't hurt the bugs. It doesn't harm any living being, take it and start sweeping."

And so the student followed the teacher's advice and started sweeping. Day and night, whenever he was awake, the student swept and swept. When people come, he sweeps the monastery. When animals come, he sweeps the monastery. All his time went into sweeping and keeping up on the dirt floor, because in those days floors were not made of concrete.

One month goes by, then two months, six months, then a year, two years, then several years pass. After sweeping every day for so long, he finally begins to see many living things crawling on the ground, running on the floor where people are walking. He tells people where to walk so they will not step on these living things. "Walk this way instead, please walk this way." But the people tell him that they don't see anything. Even his teacher cannot see what he is seeing. The student went deeply into his chore of sweeping, and he swept away all of his karma. That is what we call *right vision*.

So what happened to the student after he swept away his karma? One night when he was sweeping, he saw his teacher walking and sweeping in front of him so as not to step on any living being. The student asked him to walk a different path because there were still hundreds of living things along the path that the teacher was walking on. The teacher asked the student how he could see in the dark, revealing that this man he had considered his master had not yet attained right vision.

In contrast, without any memorized knowledge, through sweeping the student had become enlightened. You can burn away karma when you go deeply into your innocence, heart, and purity, sweeping away the darkness from karma that blocks you. The teacher was still not enlightened, but the student with the right vision, innocence, and a pure heart reached enlightenment.

When students with pure hearts and innocence ask me why they are still being blocked, the main thing I share that is blocking them is their vision. They still lack the right vision, don't know which way to go, and still need someone to guide them. Without guidance, you cannot get on the right path and achieve the right vision.

A student needs to have the right vision because they are too much in their heads. When you're too much in your head, you start to compare yourself. You begin to compare your teacher. You start to compare everything. Comparison is a significant blockage that keeps you from going into your heart.

PURITY AND EMOTIONS

All of this is easy to understand with words, but it is much more difficult in life. Purifying your heart and becoming innocent is not so simple in life. Especially when it comes to human emotions.

Feelings and emotions can create impurities of the heart if we insist on clinging to them, and people are full of them. Like anger, for example, anger is a strong emotion, but so is love. What people call love, or when they say they love this person or this animal, this is emotion. If something happened to that animal, you would begin to cry. Crying is based on emotion because without emotion crying doesn't happen.

Emotions are like *kshayas*. *Kshayas*, clouds that cover the soul, are anger, ego, deceitfulness, greediness, hate, jealousy, violence, and negativity. These are all emotions that pollute the heart. These are all impurities if held onto.

A genuine student cannot get angry. If they get angry, even if they don't show anger but it remains on the inside, they are not a real student. For real students on the path, the emotion of anger will touch them, but they don't internalize it or act on it.

So when it comes to emotions, what does a true student have to do?

You need a little soap to clean them, which is the soap of the *samyama*. Samyama means discipline. If you are disciplined and know that you need to wake up at four o'clock in the morning, no matter what happens you will wake up at four o'clock. Discipline is how people start to wash away their impurities; when they have washed them away, the pure heart is already there. We just need to clean away the pollution, like washing our clothes, faces, or bodies.

Practicing discipline washes away the impurities from your heart that have laid dormant there. Emotions like anger, jealousy, and violence are all things you need to wash away with the soap of samyama. And where do you get this soap of samyama? From the master. Like I tell my students, I am always selling the soap of samyama and tapa, or tapasya means austerity. Austerity through fasting and meditation is another way to purify your heart.

TRUTH SEEKER

A real student is a real seeker. They are always craving something unknown, which is hidden. A genuine student will always be searching for the truth and active in this pursuit. Living their life in this desired posture, they are always vibrant and full of energy. They don't just embody these attributes, they *act* on them.

The real student knows that the *sadhana*, which means one's daily spiritual practice such as chanting, meditation, and yoga is very important. Why? If anyone wants to be on the spiritual path, they have to have a sadhana because it is like medicine–we may not like it, but we still need it. But a real student will begin to crave this practice. Where there is no craving, there is no path. The spiritual path begins when there is a craving to do something for your soul. You want to wake up and learn the hidden truths inside of you.

The Jain religion has four major sects, one of which is called Sthanakvasi. The nickname for the Sthanakvasi sect's monk is *dhoondhia* which means "always searching." Now, this word is almost forgotten. I still remember when many people called Sthanakvasi monks and nuns dhoondhia - those searching for something. What were they searching for? Their soul, their truth.

Ultimately, a student has to be a seeker. They have to be interested in discovering what is missing from their life. But, once they dedicate their lives to the right path and search for the truth, they will find it if they put in the effort.

HUMILITY AND SURRENDER

Humility is also an essential quality of a real student and the root of the real path. This path doesn't take you anywhere geographically; the real path takes you into your soul.

Why is humility so important? As Mahavira shared in the first chapter of the Uttaradhyayana (Sutra), *vinayo dhammasa mulam*, which means "the root of the path is humbleness." If someone resists the path, there is ego. And where there is ego and resistance, there will be pain and suffering, and the path cannot begin or continue.

So the most crucial quality of a real student is that they are humble and seek the truth of who they are without resistance. How do they do this? It doesn't come quickly, but they must learn to dissolve their ego and surrender.

To surrender, you must not think of yourself as only being a certain way. If you do, you won't be flexible enough to endure any kind of transformation. You will be stuck in your mind. Without surrendering, a teacher or guru cannot take on a student.

Teachers have very sharp eyes, so when they see a student with potential, they understand that the student can pick the teaching up right away and they can grow. They can grow spiritually and indeed find themselves. Real teachers can see beyond what most cannot. When people see a piece of stone, a guru will see it as a diamond. That's why a teacher can see if a student has potential. They can see it in the way a person walks, in the way they talk and behave. The teacher will determine whether or not the person is real and ready.

DETACHMENT

The final main quality of a real student is non attachment. They must be completely allergic to the material trappings of the world. This shows that the student understands that these earthly things only provide temporary relief or happiness, not eternal joy. I call the real students *viraga*, which means they don't have attachments. People can progress along the path very quickly when they learn to completely detach. They become real *dhoondia, always searching*.

But how does one disentangle from worldly materialism and priorities? Spiritual practices or sadhana are essential and include reciting mantras, practicing meditation, doing yoga, fasting, and reading and understanding the scriptures or teachings of a master. As you get deeper into sadhana and embody non-attachment, you become viragi. You might live in the world, but the world doesn't live in you. Once viragi happens, your path quickly begins to improve drastically. You will see how fast you grow and discover your soul.

Non-attachment is very simple to talk about but much more challenging to live because many people struggle with this concept and it needs to be more widely understood. Attachment doesn't mean you are a millionaire or own many beautiful houses. You can have all those things and not be attached as long as you are not identified with them. You can be attached and identify with wealth even if you only have one dollar, or jewelry, or whatever it is that you are giving so much meaning to.

People do terrible things because of attachment. They lie and cheat. They steal and kill. People die because of attachment. Attachment is a killer, and detachment makes you free. If you have everything and do not need it or self-identify with it, that's non-attachment.

Detachment means you only take what you need to survive, for example like the food you eat to survive. If your body is not alive, then you cannot do sadhana. Your body has to be active, and when your body is alive, you can do more sadhana, fasting, and good for humanity. As humans, we eat to survive, but attachment comes when we crave food, eat more than we need, and eat animals for pleasure. We must eat to be alive because our body needs it to live. We must eat, not just consume. There are ways to become detached from food. It takes practice.

Anything can be an attachment, but family, food, and material things are the most difficult. Each of these can keep you away from the path, and you can have difficulty letting them go.

Detachment includes sexual relationships. In Parshvanath's time, women were thought of as possessions, as things. That's why Parshvanath didn't make five of the mahavratas (great vows). He only made four mahavratas. Chaturyam, which means four mahavratas. This is because celibacy was not separated as a spiritual guideline for monks. Why? Because back then, women were not seen as equals. They were treated as possessions. So they saw "non-possession" already implied celibacy since detachment would mean that men couldn't have women and women couldn't have men. Those were backward times. Now it's widely understood that we are all equal. So now, we have five mahavratas, established by Mahavir, because possessions and celibacy are separated into two vows.

Attachment to anything can block your path, but attachment to people can be one of the hardest to break. This is often called *raga* but most misunderstand the meaning of it. They believe that attachment is love, but that's not true. Attachment and love are separate. Raga is lethal. It is a spiritual block that will not allow you to walk on your path.

LOVE

Remember all these qualities are usually not something we are born with. We must develop them. But to develop these qualities, they must have devotion and be full of love. Loving devotion inspires a person to dedicate their lives to the spiritual path, the right path.

Having love and devotion helps you improve upon these qualities you are not born with. When you know how to love yourself, you can love others too. But if you don't love yourself, you can't truly love others either. When love for self and others is purified, it can be Godly love, divine love. When emotional love is refined, it becomes Godly love.

Real students will dedicate their lives to the path just like others dedicate their lives to their families and careers. Of course, it takes time to improve these qualities, but anybody anywhere can become a real student if they spend time working on themselves. You will become more vigorous and robust if you step on the right path, and Godly love will help you stay on that path.

WHY

Spiritual Teachers
in Ancient Traditions

PART II

Chapter 6 —

Differentiating between True and False Teachers

In the previous chapters, I've shared qualities of what it means to be a real student, and one of the most significant is being able to surrender to the teacher.

Now, the question is this. With millions of teachers worldwide, how do you know if you're surrendering to the right one? How do you know if a master is truly a master or if a teacher is a genuine spiritual teacher? A teacher has to be authentic and genuine because if you find a random teacher it is easy to get fooled by a big following or a mesmerizing personality; thus, knowing how to identify a real teacher is very important.

False teachers have been around since the beginning, even since Mahavira's time. Five or six other teachers were more popular than Mahavira, but they were known for not teaching the right thing. One of their names is Ajit Kesakambali. He had a mesmerizing personality, and many people followed him. Another one was Prabuddha Katyaya, who was also very popular. The third one was Sanjay Vilethiputta, who was so renowned for his logic and convincing arguments that many people forgot about Mahavira. Finally, Goshalak was the most popular of them all, but they were all fake teachers. Even Buddha competed in the Tirthankaras race but never became a Tirthankara even though some people claimed he was one. Amongst all of these other teachers, Mahavira was probably the most quiet and unassuming. But in the end, who was left as a Tirthankara? Mahavira was.

SIGNS OF AN UNENLIGHTENED TEACHER

If you see someone with a big crowd around them or who holds their audience's rapt attention with compelling speeches, you might think they are a real teacher, but no. A real teacher might only talk to you a little. Then, maybe in silence, he or she might tell you everything. It's tough because sometimes what the real teacher teaches and the fake teacher teaches can sound identical. However, a real teacher will not do certain things.

For example, the real teacher will not get involved in politics or be a politician. To me, politics is a dirty game. And likewise, politicians cannot be spiritual teachers. Many people are blind and do not realize that Gandhi never claimed that he was a spiritual teacher. Instead he was always telling people that he was a politician. He worked for political change. Maybe along the way his motivations changed, but he never claimed he was a spiritual teacher. So he was at least truthful about it.

You can also identify real teachers by their physical behavior. If somebody's going to the gym, making their body strong, and trying to mesmerize people with their muscles, those are not the actions of a sincere teacher. When people are fully immersed in spirituality, they don't have or want to use any extra time playing golf, riding motorcycles, or spending hours in a gym. Those are not symptoms of a real teacher. The real teachers have achieved what they're supposed to have achieved and don't have to show their body or personality or this or that to do it. They are focused less on the body (although they certainly live healthy as we will discuss in a later chapter) and more on the soul.

The spiritual teacher's eyes will look calm, like there's nothing in it. Like when you see a baby's eyes, what do you see? They are pure. They are blank slates. But a mesmerizing teacher's eyes tell you something different. They try to show that "Hey, I can drink the poison, and I will not die." They will do things to try to convince you that they are real. They will put the venom in milk and tell you they can drink it without being harmed, but that is all for the show, all for ego.

The real teacher doesn't try to prove that they are real, but fake teachers are always trying to, which is the main problem. They might say, "If you hug me, I will heal you." But a real teacher doesn't embrace or touch people for healing. Maybe they're so compassionate that they might hug someone here and there. A real teacher won't spend ten hours hugging each person in a big crowd. No, that is showing off. I've seen this in India with certain "spiritual teachers" and how students become so enchanted by a teacher's hug or blessing that they don't realize that what they are feeding off of is more excitement than enlightenment. A student must learn to differentiate between enthusiasm for a *teacher* and a real sense of peace derived from the *teachings*.

I have also seen in India how people can become so mesmerized by fake teachers who lie down naked on thorns to make people think they are authentic. I once witness a swami take something out of his mouth that he claimed came from his stomach, it was just a magic trick while pretending to manifest things. Fake teachers will show you something that will make you think, "How did they manifest this?" But it's all a trick. You don't see that they are reaching their hand into their pocket. It's like a trick of the hands, an illusion. But unfortunately, too many people find themselves mesmerized by the mystery or showmanship of fake teachers. But what do these "teachers" do at night? They smoke ganja, bhang, marijuana, or other drugs and are practicing no spiritual behaviors whatsoever. But the crowds don't see that part, and that's how they can get deceived.

Therefore, you must be careful with fake teachers who have been around since the beginning. Unfortunately, millions and millions of counterfeit spiritual teachers think they can teach better than real teachers. Sometimes people get trapped in it and get astray. Therefore, the student has to be wise enough to find a genuine teacher.

THE ENLIGHTENED TEACHER AS SOURCE ITSELF

Once you achieve the highest state of consciousness and know that truth is coming from you, there's just no meaning in doing those things. Truth doesn't come from books. So if somebody claims they are real spiritual teachers and use books all the time, they cannot have their own pure experiences. That person is a scholar, not a spiritual teacher.

A scholar can narrate, explain and comment on the Gita, or the Bible, but it doesn't mean they are a spiritual teacher. A spiritual teacher is someone who becomes experienced or self-realized. And when somebody is realized, everything comes from their inner consciousness. The whole knowledge is hidden there, and you don't have to read the book. A spiritual teacher might quote from a book, but not solely base their teachings off of it.

The real spiritual teacher is different. They're primarily in a meditative state. They speak when needed; otherwise, they are silent, and you feel a certain peace around them.

That peace hits the center part of your body, your aura, your navel, your third chakra.

Once you feel it in your third chakra, your energy will blossom as you explore a spiritual teacher. Whether or not the spiritual teacher teaches you or not teaches, you will still feel this peace radiate from them.

Real teachers are rare. You must remember that you can travel hundreds or thousands of miles and still not find the real teacher. It is challenging because a real teacher is very simple. They are down to earth. And they desire to share everything they know with students. This knowledge comes from deep within their being, as direct knowledge always comes from the bottom of your soul. Indirect knowledge comes through studying books. Although books may affect teachers, their actual knowledge is drawn from the deepest wells of one's soul. Here is where the absolute truth lives.

SIGNS OF AN ENLIGHTENED TEACHER

When people ask me how a person can differentiate between excitement around a teacher and feeling peace, feeling the truth, I say this. Excitement is something that happens within your physical body. It is a temporary feeling. When a person gets excited, it happens momentarily, and then after a while the excitement will go away. You can even put the teacher to the test and see if your feelings are still the same after a prolonged period of being away from them. Something needs to be addressed when a person gets too excited by a teacher. A mesmerizing personality is a big red flag. Look at Hitler. He was so mesmerizing. He made fools of thousands of people and inspired them to be violent.

I can tell you one tangible example of a teacher in India. He's behind bars now. His name is Ram Rahim, and he was so widely known and respected that even all the politicians would bow down to him.

But Ram Rahim was a drunk driver. So who made him a famous guru? Many ignorant and foolish people are the ones who make these kinds of gurus possible. They are not real seekers but rather blind followers who wanted desperately to believe this man could create miracles in their lives. Fake teachers are created by people who allow themselves to be fooled. Without people willing to believe in them, fake teachers could not exist. Therefore, fake teachers are the creation of the fool.

Real teachers don't even consider themselves high or awakened. They just teach and guide people. They try to lift souls. They guide people higher. And mostly, real teachers lift people when they are in their presence. They don't have to show anything. Their teachings are so simple and humble. Lao Tzu was a Chinese enlightened master who lived around 2600 to 2800 years ago. When he was dying a thousand students were sitting around him, and one student asked him, "We have known you for many years, and as long as we have known you, we've never seen anybody push you down. What is your secret? How come nobody has ever pushed you down."

And to this, Lao Tzu said, "I was always sitting on the ground."

If you are sitting on the ground, who will push you down?

Many students laughed, but it was real. He was down to earth. When you are down to earth, nobody can push you down.

The real teacher is difficult to find. How many Mahaviras can you find? How many Lao Tzus can you find? Only one. With real teachers it is about quality, not quantity. And so, with all quality things, they are scarce. For example, there are millions of Buddhist monks and nuns, but they don't always have quality. But in the Jain religion, one of the world's oldest religions, there are only 12,000 monks and nuns worldwide. Quality usually lacks in quantity, but dominates in its ability.

Chapter 7 —

Leaving Religion for Spirituality

In this chapter, I will share how you can transition from religion into spirituality. This is a question many people have.

The transition from religion to spirituality happens by experience. If a person doesn't go through an incident that provokes this, the change may never occur. Buddha's case is an example of this, because he encountered a lot of false teachings before his transition into spirituality. One teacher taught the practice of hanging a huge stone by your ear's lobes while meditating. No matter how much pain you were in, you could not move while you meditated like this. Buddha did as the teacher said because he was only sixteen years old and didn't know anything about life yet. He kept going until he realized it was killing his body. It was negative experiences like this that convinced him that he could find a better way. No matter how many teachers he met, no one taught *the truth*.

Eventually he was initiated into the Samanic tradition, which caused him to start meditating and practicing Kayotsarga (a meditation technique focused on detaching from your body) by sitting under the tree. After some time, he finally experienced a glimpse of real truth and had his big awakening. Awakening is different from enlightenment.

REASONS FOR SPIRITUAL TRANSITION

Transition happens because a person has certain life experiences that push them away from religion. If they don't have these, they will get stuck in religion. Religion is a beautiful thing, but it is also a curse. Most religions are based in fear, and we cannot improve ourselves because of fear. When fear controls our thoughts, it will create so much anxiety and bring worries into our lives that we cannot eliminate that fear. Religion will tell you that if you don't follow it, you will go to hell, and that's the greatest fear of all, right? So perpetual fear keeps people stuck in religion.

What type of vision does religion give you? Religion is like trying to see outside while looking through a keyhole. How much can you look at that way? Not very much. Why? Because religion is often a big mess. When you read about world history, most wars and conflicts happened because of religion. Even when religion creates chaos and wars, violence and hate, people will still follow it. Religion has many followers, even though it is messy.

When people move away from religion, they begin to follow their intuition, and intuition tells you the truth. That's why transition is natural. It's like you become allergic to the old teacher, or you become allergic to the teacher's source. Only then are you ready to embrace something new.

I have met a lot of people who come to our retreat and share similar stories. They say how they were raised Catholic but grew apart from the church and in essence they became "allergic" to it. When I ask them why, they share the same things repeatedly: You cannot doubt the church or ask questions. In the beginning of your life it all seemed real and true. But as you grow, if you cannot have doubt or ask questions - how can somebody clear your mind?

They tell me that's why they are seeking meditation. They are seeking some kind of yoga, some kind of breathing, some type of other things that gives them some guidance and divine experience. And fortunately, most of the people we are meeting now are not religious. They are more interested in what we call spirituality.

Spirituality is like an open sky. You can see everything from the north to the south, from the east to the west. Religion only shows you one direction, and it's like that tiny view through a keyhole. That limited vision is why people get stuck and feel they cannot get out. But if you're like a bird, you will fly and can see the whole world. You are free.
Who is free? Those who don't have fear. That's freedom. But people who have fear are not free at all.

OVERCOMING GUILT FOR THE SPIRITUAL PATH

Guilt is the biggest sin. If somebody is carrying guilt, they are carrying the sin. Guilt is too heavy for the heart to bear.

Catholics believe in confession, so Catholic priests have a confessional that people come to that is a private booth with a little window and curtain over it where a person sits and can disclose their sins privately.

The priest will say, "Oh, my child, what do you need to tell me?"

And the person begins to say, "I did this sin, I made this mistake, I lied, I hurt someone, I cheated."

Then the priest will say, "My child, God is very compassionate. God forgives you. Do this penance and your sins will be removed."

And they believe in God and hope God forgives them because now the priests told them that God forgives them. This kind of removal of guilt is only temporary, but that guilt (or karma) will never be wiped out. Confession in Catholicism is temporary relief, but the sin or karma is still there.

Many do not know that Jesus learned in the eastern countries, primarily India. Somehow, he got this confession system from the Jains, but Catholics don't realize where Jesus got the idea of confession. The only problem is, when Jesus taught about confession, he didn't teach the whole practice.

Jains still practice confession the way it's supposed to be done. According to Jainism, when the priest says that God forgives you, that is not enough. It doesn't wipe out your guilt. The person has to deal with what they did, and it comes with the punishment. It is taking full responsibility for one's own actions. If you don't punish the person, their guilt will never be wiped out.

I once met a woman from Bangalore in South India who told me how she suffered a tremendous amount of guilt. She told me that she could not sleep, eat, or drink because of it. She wanted to confess and tell me what had happened, but she was in India and could not come to the United States.

She found me on my website and thought I might be able to help wipe out her guilt.

I asked her what her confession was. She told me that she had two children but unexpectedly got pregnant a third time. She knew that once her husband found out, he would not allow her to keep the baby. She wanted to have this child, but her family and her husband's family pressured her into aborting it. Everyone told her that two children were enough, especially as this third child was a girl. So they convinced her to terminate her pregnancy even though she did not want to. So, under the weight of her family's influence, she aborted the baby. She felt like she killed the baby and that her guilt would never go away. She couldn't sleep or find peace; the responsibility was always with her. She wanted a real confession.

I told her I would give her the real confession and punishment if she was ready to do it. I told her, "Your punishment begins tomorrow. You must go to the orphanage and find a little girl to adopt and raise as your own child."

I knew her family would be against this idea, so I advised her to talk to an attorney first. "You must have divorce papers ready. As soon as you bring the girl home, your family will be against you, but they cannot push you if you have an attorney already. If you're ready to do it today and adopt a little girl, I guarantee it will wipe out your guilt completely, but that is your punishment." She got the courage. She did what I said and secretly hired a lawyer, while her family had no idea what she was doing.

Finally, one day, she came home with a baby girl who was maybe three or four months old. Someone had left their baby out in the streets, but now she had a mother. As soon as she entered the house with this baby girl in her arms, hell broke loose. Everybody was against her—her husband, parents, brothers, and sister. I told her she must not care about what they think or do. If they start to yell or hit her, she must call the police. But after only one month, the whole situation began to change. They all fell in love with this little girl. When she called me to give me an update, she said, "Guess what? They all fell in love with the baby. Now, I can finally sleep, eat, and feel relaxed."

Catholicism doesn't have this type of punishment after a confession. The woman never felt guilty after that. Why? Because now she's raising what is not hers. This is an example of how guilt can be wiped out.

The transition into genuine confession takes work. It will bring guilt, and guilt is the biggest killer. Only the Samanic tradition offers real confession with a punishment to wipe out someone's guilt. The punishment is always in accordance with the confession.

Why have guilt in transition from religion to spirituality? Spirituality means freedom. Don't feel guilty about leaving an old box.

OPENING UP TO SPIRITUALITY

In my experience, when students come to me, they do not carry any guilt at all but want to learn. I ask if they are coming from a certain religion and how many other teachers they have had. If they say, for example, they've had twenty teachers before me and I will be the twenty-first, I know they will compare my teachings to everything they have learned. Whatever I say to them, they will compare it to the past and never learn from me. So the best thing I can do is help them transition. I warn them that while the transition is happening that they must leave everything they've previously learned behind them.

Be a blank slate so that whatever I write on the blank slate has a chance to become real. If a student compares what I say to other teachers, then someone else is the right person to teach them. If I know that they intend to compare, or to only learn just a little bit, I will not teach them. I will not answer their questions. If your goal is to compare and cling to past beliefs, then your goal of enlightenment will never happen because your intention is not to learn.

However, most students do not come with messy slates. Their heart is like a baby's heart. This way I can mold them, whatever I say they're going to do. They will go into a meditative state or spiritual sadhana as they adopt spiritual practices. So that's how I will teach; otherwise, teaching is difficult.

All students carry their own mess to clean up, but if they are ready to become real students, I can teach them. Once I know they are authentic and open, I will find a way to help them.

Chapter 8 —

Jainism: Teaching Religion or Spirituality?

In this chapter I go into great depth about the Jain system and how it interplays with the differences between religion and spirituality. Some people might think that I am a Jain teacher, but I don't really teach. Instead, I prefer to say I like to share. I don't see myself as a Jain teacher. I am just as I am. I know I mention Jainism a lot when speaking because Jainism is one branch of Samanic Tradition and has the teachings of the Tirthankaras, extraordinary enlightened masters, and are not found in any other religion. Out of all religions, it holds the most truth in regards to spirituality.

Currently, Jainism is the only branch which is closest to the Samanic Tradition. All the other traditions or branches are diminished, or have disappeared. For example, there was an offshoot called the Sankhya System, which has all but disappeared as well. The same thing has happened within Buddhism. There was the original system of Buddhism, that has almost completely disappeared. Whatever Buddhism today is not the same as the original teachings.

The closest thing to the Samanic Tradition is solely Jainism. But we must remember that the Samanic Tradition was not a religion. The Tirthankaras never taught any religion at all because they did not want to add one more branch and keep people in a box. Their teachings reflect freedom.

This is why Tirthankaras are considered universal. Their teachings are universal. But as soon as any branch becomes an organized religion, it spoils the teachings. This is why I have difficulty with the concept that I'm a Jain teacher because it confines the teachings and is not universal anymore. Then you become a Jain, and Jain is a box. But Jainism is only a little branch of Tirthankara teachings, and those are for the universe. Anybody can follow the Tirthankaras' teachings, but it is unfortunate that the Jain tradition has become unknown to most people. Tirthankara is supposed to be known to everyone. It used to be.

That's why I thought it is better not to belong to any religion, I teach more overall spirituality. Spirituality is hidden in every single religion more or less, but I mention Jainism more because there is so much truth hidden within that tradition and it needs to be revealed again.

Hinduism is another religion that seems to have borrowed much of their system from the Samanic Tradition. Their most popular book, called the Bhagavad Gita, also has spirituality hidden within a couple of its chapters. It is collected from the Samanic Tradition too, because it contains bhakti (devotional) yoga, gyan (knowledge) yoga, and karma (service) yoga.

Most religions follow some form of the truth. But many of them create new additions and distance themselves from the original truth. For example, there are only thirteen original Upanishads, and even the Hindus believe that Adi Shankaracharya wrote only eleven authentic commentaries on the Upanishads. Hindus consider him as the founder of Hinduism and also kind of like a God to them. Buddhists think otherwise about Adi Shankaracharya because he burned down their monasteries and all of the Indian literature that the Buddhists were protecting. There is no spirituality in that. Circling back, there are more and more additions to the original text.

One example is the Allah Upanishad. This was added to the original text to reflect the Islam invasion into India. It already shows its going further and further away from the original writings. There is some truth hidden in the original thirteen Upanishads, anything outside of that is far from the truth.

The Samanic teachings were passed down orally. They were not written, but rather passed from guru to disciple, and then disciple to another disciple. The tradition was to memorize to preserve the teachings. Unfortunately, like anything that gets passed down and sometimes failed memories, the original teachings are lost. Even when you pass something down between three people, the message gets muddled. The originality of the Tirthankaras' teachings got lost; however, 10% of truth is still available in the Jain scriptures. That is a lot.

THREE POWERFUL JAIN TEACHINGS

The last Tirthankara was Mahavir and he was an extraordinary person. All Tirthankaras are extraordinary people on the earth, but what he used to teach in particular is why I am most drawn to the Jain branch. There are three particular beliefs that attract me the most.

One is their slogan, the first slogan is *parasparopagraho jivanam*. If you see the Jain branch logo, pratik they call it, it is written underneath parasparopagraho jivanam. Co-existence. Co-existence means you let others live and then you live. But Jains twisted it, they say live and let live. It reflects that they're selfish people. They think about themselves. First live, then *let* live. The Tirthankara never said that. They said *let live* first. Live, when others live, you already exist, but if you don't respect others, or you kill others, and you hurt them, or you don't protect them, it means you are not protected either. That slogan attracted me a lot: to co-exist and live in harmony.

The second powerful teaching is the multiplicity of truth, also known as *Anekantavada*. Truth can be told many different ways. It's a multiplicity of truth. There is always a substance of truth in everything. If people follow this in the world today, there would be no fighting and no wars, because there would be an understanding between two parties. To listen and consider the other person's point of view and see where they are coming from instead of declaring you are the only one that is right. Living by these teachings reduces ego in the world. Although absolute truth cannot be spoken, truth can be considered from multiple points of view.

Lao Tse once said, "The dao (truth), which can be told, is not the dao." It means the truth cannot be told. That is what the multiplicity of truth is. Any person can be right in their own way. It's not that they are absolutely true and correct, but they can be truthful from their point of view. We have to understand, consider, and respect each other's point of view.

Even a murderer can be very truthful. Forget the good people. Even the bad people can be truthful too, because they see only that much. They see maybe their own way of the truth. It's very hard, but if we follow the multiplicity of truth then we will see why this person has killed others. That means this person needs help. Maybe they are not seeing the way it's supposed to be seen. We need to be willing to help that person. Why is this person drinking too much? Maybe they have some problem, so we have to help them. If we follow this, this is the universal system. Multiplicity of truth is in the Tirthankaras teachings.

I'm also attracted to *Syadvada* in the Jain system. Siyadvada is also called *Sapt Bhangi Nyaya* or *Saapekshvada*, which is the theory of relativity. And that's why I respect Mahavir a lot because he shared this theory. He modified it from the Samanic Tradition and he made it saapekshvada, the theory of relativity and who gets credit for this? Albert Einstein. Albert Einstein stole this theory, saapekshvada, from India and people consider him as a genius. The Germans worked on translating the Jain scriptures and he came across it. He's widely known for the theory, but the original person was Tirthankar Mahavir, who mentioned and taught it over 2,600 years ago. Maybe people need to rewrite history again about who stole this extraordinary person's theory of relativity. Similarly, Gandhi gets credit as the apostle of non-violence, when he was mainly teaching what Tirthankar Mahavir taught. In reality, it is the Tirthankaras who are the apostles of non-violence because that's what they preached.

I like the Jain branch a lot and mention it often. It contains so many treasures that are lost in the present-day or people get credit for those who are not the original ones. There is nothing new to discover about spirituality, the foundation is there in the Jain system, but one must be wise not to get stuck in the religion, but rather take the jewels of spirituality from it.

I consider myself more of a Samanic teacher than a Jain one. The Samanic tradition was the original and it has spirituality. At least with the Jain system some of the Samanic teachings are preserved, especially through their scriptures.

I try to teach people spirituality. Spirituality means to get connected with yourself and at the same time you get connected with everyone. Once you get connected to the whole universe, your spirituality begins, but if you are not connected, you don't love and respect the vegetation, the animals, the stars, the moon, then how do you expect to feel "oneness with the universe." It's easy to say and declare, but to practice requires improving and purifying yourself. As you help yourself, you help others.

Spirituality is supposed to be the most courageous path with profound teachings to improve yourself. That's why I teach spirituality instead of one branch of spirituality only. Even though Jainism has 10% truth hidden in it, I will still suggest you study their scriptures, because whatever is there is still valuable. Jainism, compared to all other religions, holds the most truth today. It's unfortunate, not many people know about it.

The Samanic Tradition is the Tirthankara Tradition - we need more of that. The teachings need to be expanded and shared once again, because it is universal and for everyone, regardless of where they are on their journey.

Chapter 9 —

Tirthankaras: The Extraordinary Enlightened Masters

The last chapter discussed the Jain system and what Jainism is. Then, I briefly touched on the souls known as the Tirthankaras. I mentioned they were extraordinary beings and revolutionary, but who are the Tirthankaras? In this chapter, I will elaborate on their purpose and how we can all benefit from their teachings today. Tirthankara is a Sanskrit word, and it is a great word. The Prakrit word is Tiththayar. It is the same as Tirthankara and the Sanskrit version is what became popular.

According to the Sanskrit language, "Tirtham karoti iti Tirthankara." The person who makes a harbor to cross the ocean of suffering. Tirtham is a harbor. It's symbolic.

Also, there are four tirthas, or in this aspect, pillars in the Jain system. The sadhu and sadhvi (monks and nuns), and shravak and shravika (the spiritual householders). They are also a kind of tirtha because they are all boarded into the ship. However, the ship needs to stay somewhere, where to board, a safe harbor. As I mentioned, tirtham means harbor. So a Tirthankara is a person who creates a safe harbor for those who are suffering to board the ship and cross the ocean of suffering. By translation that is what Tirthankara means, but a Tirthankara is extraordinary and exceptional too.

Tirthankara Gotra is somebody who has the karma and destiny to be a Tirthankara. This is a very rare soul. They have to have an abundance of punya and mahapunya-type karmic particles. Mahapunya means abundance of punya, virtues. They have collected a lot of virtues in their previous lives. That makes them special and exceptional people in this universe. When they're born, they are born with three types of knowledge: mati jnana, shruti jnana, and avadhi jnana. Mati jnana is higher intelligence, shruti jnana is intelligence through hearing, and avadhi jnana means they can see a lot more than a typical human, like one thousand miles or ten thousand miles away without blockage. They have the ability, at birth, to see through walls.

They can see through as I am looking at you the same way. In general, they don't get too involved in the household affairs. For example, most of them don't get married, or they don't have children, but it's not the rule though. Many people think it is the rule that all Tirthankaras are born fully formed and remain the same way as a child.

There have been twenty-four Tirthankaras on this planet, in a previous era. Earth is considered a lucky planet because it is able to have Tirthankara energy.

The first Tirthankara, Adinath, married Chakravarthi Shanthinath. He was married, and they had children. It shows that there is not a rule that a Tirthankara cannot be married, though when they renounce to become a monk, they renounce all. There is no set rule that they cannot have children or have a householder's life. They are still exceptional in many ways. Their extraordinary bodies contain all the best particles collected from the whole universe.

That's what makes them extraordinary people. So I'm using a person because they still have a body. It is the last body. It's a fantastic body. It's like the best particle, and when it is the best particle, can you believe the mother, how advanced spiritually she is to bear a child with Tirthankar particles? She had the best karma to bear an extraordinary person. She must also have had an abundance of punya or virtues. So she has collected a lot of good karma. When a Tirthankara comes, there's peace around the world automatically. Sometimes people have the view that a Tirthankara is like a superhuman.

They are superhuman in the sense of being extraordinary, they are almost like living Gods in a human body. They possess all the knowledge of God, and their body is different. Their body has thirty-four *athishya*, which means wonderful things, people say miracles, happen all the time around them which common humans don't experience. They are also unique because they speak thirty-five kinds of languages, which everybody understands. Even animals understand them. It is hard to find that kind of person on the earth, but they're born as a human. They're born, and they live as humans. They go to school just like other people. Enlightened ones have the same higher consciousness as a Tirthankara, but the Tirthankara is considered higher only because of their strong, revolutionary body type. Knowledge, enlightenment, and awakening is the same. An enlightened one would bow to a Tirthankara.

As soon as they renounce the world, they achieve their destiny as a Tirthankara. They've collected so much virtue in past lives. Usually, they are born into a special family that is well-off, prosperous, and in good health. It is that kind of family they chose.

They also have amazing bodies that weapons or bullets cannot break. If a bullet touches a Tirthankara's body, it will just slip by. It doesn't go inside their body because their body is so strong. In the Jain system, they call it *vajra rishabh naaraach sanghanan*. The body's structure is so strong that the body is like a vajra. Vajra is something that cannot be broken, like a diamond. It's called a vajra diamond. If you put a vajra diamond on a thick piece of steel and strike it with a sledgehammer, you won't break it. Instead, it will go into the steel. The Tirthankara's body is like that, and their body cannot be broken.

What is the purpose of the Tirthankaras? The truth is their purpose is no purpose. Their purpose is whatever we imagine it to be. Their purpose is to help people. They have already crossed the ocean of suffering and can help others travel the spiritual path too. That's what their purpose is. Otherwise, they know teaching doesn't help. It is our illusion that this exceptional teacher, this master, is coming to help. No, that's not it. If your karma or other people's karma is not ready to learn to observe, even if God is right in front of you, you cannot be straightened out. Tirthankaras bodies are unique because they contain the best particles in the universe. All those particles are collected in their human body so that they can create a miracle around them.

This is why incredible things happen naturally around them. Their energy cultivates in their country of birth and makes it become more peaceful. Where they are, there will be less crime for many years. Their energy will leave a positive impact for thousands of years. Even one thousand years after they pass, their energy will still affect people. The Tirthankaras were born in India and surrounding areas. Although the Jain system holds their teachings, the Tirthankaras taught spirituality, not religion. Unfortunately, the Jains have made their teachings a religion. Where their teachings are meant to inspire people to become free. The box of religion was created out of fear not to lose the teachings.

In the Jain system, they call Tirthankaras a live God because they cannot communicate with the real God - the real God is shapeless. There needs to be more communication. You can realize only God. But with the Tirthankara, you can contact them and connect with them, but you have to be in a special meditative state. You can still connect with the Tirthankara, and as I mentioned previously, there are only so many planets that can bear that kind of energy - these are the luckiest planets. In the whole universe, which has millions of galaxies, only one hundred and seventy are the luckiest planets. They can bear those kinds of powerful, high energy. Other planets might just get blown away, but our Earth is one of the lucky ones. One hundred and sixty-nine other planets in the whole universe can be a home to Tirthankaras. 20 planets always have a Tirthankara. So a minimum of 20 Tirthankaras are always available at any given time. At the time of writing this book, there are 20 Tirthankaras today throughout the universe. We can communicate with them, even though they're not on our planet. But you have to be in that mode.

We call them *virahmaan,* and according to the Jain system, one of the oldest known Tirthankaras is Simandhar Swami. Simandhar Swami is one out of the twenty right now and is quite popular. He is in Mahavideh. Mahavideh is one of the planets in the universe, not in this galaxy, that can host a Tirthankara. We can connect with him and the others by deep meditation.

Arihanta, an enlightened master, is a living God because they've achieved that state, but not all enlightened masters are Tirthankaras, but all Tirthankaras are enlightened masters.

Out of curiosity, several students have asked me how many enlightened ones today are on Earth? They are challenging to find, but if you ask me today at the time of this writing, they can be counted on one hand and most don't speak English. Sometimes people get enlightenment and die right away because they cannot take the energy, their body cannot handle it, and it is ok - their goal was achieved.

People can claim they are a master, but when you visit them, you find something else. People used to say Jiddu Krishnamurti was a master. But if you read his works, it is a combination of spirituality and psychology and is more intellectual. If somebody can express themselves very well, it doesn't mean they're enlightened or a master. They can be a master in different ways - maybe they've mastered their compassion, or anger, or ego, but it doesn't mean they have the highest knowledge like an enlightened one.

Just becoming someone who can recite from holy books doesn't mean they are a master. Maybe they are scholars. The Arihanta and Tirthankara are on that level. Of course, they are the same, but still, Tirthankara is an extraordinary exception.

There is no discrimination. Anybody can be a Tirthankara. On this earth, out of twenty-four Tirthankaras, one was female according to the Shwetambar sect in Jainism, which has the most followers.

They are spreading the message of Tirthankaras everywhere. The Digambar sect cannot do it because they're naked monks. According to Shwetambar sects, all three groups under Shwetambars believe Mallinath, the 19th Tirthankara, was Mallibai. They believe, they clearly say in their scripture, that she was a female, born female, and became a Tirthankara even as a female. Anyone who says that women cannot be Tirthankaras doesn't respect females, and I don't like those people, no matter who they are. We are all equal. Our body is made in the same way. Our body is a combination of male and female. Our body is also made by the male and by the female. So there is no significant difference, only little differences like a few organs separate males and females. This doesn't make females lower than males - they are the same. That's why a Tirthankara can be a female or a male. I fully support that idea. I disagree with the Digambar sect, which doesn't believe in equality. They don't support that a female can be enlightened (that it only happens to males) and they don't support that the 19th Tirthankara was a female, and instead was male. It's backward thinking and untrue. I'm not saying that because I was initiated into the Shwetambar sect. I consider myself sectless. I'm not religious, I'm spiritual. She was Mallibai and she was an amazing Tirthankara and her teachings were bold for the time period she lived in.

It's interesting, on the outside of the Jain temple, there is a message on the wall that says, "We believe in Truth." And yet, what is inside, they make it Mallinath - a male version of the female Tirthankara. The truth is, she was a female, it needs to be accepted, and it is the message that even Tirthankara believes in equality. They don't discriminate against anything, anybody.

In the past, I've talked about not worshiping statues and going to temples and these sorts of things for the reason that the statues are not gods themselves, but instead represent the teachings, qualities of the master. However, some people might get turned off by the ideas of temples and worshiping statues because they have left religion for spirituality. Here's what I would say about that. These statues are symbolic because when they started making statues of Tirthankaras, there was a purpose behind them. After all, there was no writing system. Their followers, the Tirthankaras' students, thought about how they could keep their teachings alive for thousands of years. So they created a statue and started to identify each Tirthankara by their symbol. You will notice the statues look the same, but what differentiates them are their symbols. For the first Tirthankara, Adinath, his symbol was the bull. He is also known as Rishabhdev and Adishwar.

Rishabh means bull. That was his central teaching because, in those days the bull was considered a very innocent animal. The bull helped the farmer by carrying all the weight of the produce. When a bull is thirsty, he will still go to the destination, but all the other animals will not. You try a horse. If a horse gets thirsty, he will not keep going. A bull will carry as far as he can and would rather die, but he will not take you or stop only halfway. He will strive to maintain his strength everywhere, and go as far as he needs to. So that is his symbol. It represents the strength, the attitude of never giving up, and the innocence and simplicity of the people during that time period. Even if you need to eat and there's no food or water around, you keep going. You never leave your path. You're stubborn, like a bull, and be steady on your path. His main teaching was simple, be innocent and you have chances to realize God.

So if you see the statues of the Tirthankaras, to me they seem more like female, not male, by the features of the face; however, you can also consider that the Tirthankaras are pregnant with infinite wisdom. They are carrying the whole universe in their body.

I firmly tell people that everything is symbolic as to why they started making the statues. All the Tirthankaras have different symbols reflecting their main teaching or the time period of when they exist and the mentality of that society. When they pay respect to Tirthankaras, they're paying respect to their teachings. That was the idea when establishing temples and their statues. Not to worship the Tirthankaras and limiting them to a stone. It's more like visiting a memorial and appreciating their teachings. They're honoring their knowing. That's what it is. When you sit in the temple of Tirthankaras, you have that feeling: Hey, I want to go deep like them so I can be enlightened. I can be pregnant. So pregnant with the whole universe, knowing that's what it is.

All Tirthankaras are pregnant, no matter whether they are male or female.

A PAST LIFE EXPERIENCE WITH A TIRTHANKAR

In the last section, we discussed the Tirthankaras and how amazing they are. We go even deeper into the subject of Tirthankaras because it's essential to know about the revolutionary enlightened masters whose teachings still influence us today. Tirthankaras are unknown to people, but if we don't learn about them, they will be unknown forever. People often wonder what kind of karma it takes for a student to learn from a Tirthankara, because there is such a limited number of Tirthankaras living in any era. I will share my experience about what it was like learning from a Tirthankara, which most people don't know about.

Things can only be revealed when they are asked for. If you don't ask the questions, you won't receive the answers. That's why I always say - ask. People always need to ask because when you do, there will be more clarity, even if it's just a little bit.

As I mentioned, Tirthankaras have a special body. It seems like the embodied God in it. The best particles in the universe. Can you believe that all of the best particles of the universe can be found in just one body? That's a Tirthankara.

To be a student of Tirthankara also requires an abundance of punya (virtues). Abundance means mountain-high punya. It means you've done phenomenal work and collected many virtues. If somebody visits a Tirthankara before, even listening to them, can you believe how *punyashali*, how lucky they are? Even animals who get to be close to a Tirthankara are fortunate and virtuous. One of the best things about the Tirthankara is how they are a magnet for all living things. Every animal will understand the Tirthankaras' teaching in their way, even the goat sitting there. The goat will understand. In the present moment, God can seem like an animal body that people don't know. This goat can be a precious, particular person in the next life. It may be guiding and teaching thousands of people. But people just see only the present. They need to see further what is going to happen.

To be a student of the Tirthankara in the human body is more valuable because the human body has a mind. The mind can grasp a lot of things, and the mind pours everything into the heart. Everything goes to the core.

I was a disciple of the 23rd Tirthankara of this era. His name was Parshvanath. He was born in Varanasi. It's a remarkable city. It still is, and his palace is still there. It's ruined, but they are keeping it. They keep repairing it. They made a temple there. He was born into a royal family, which was very special. When I visited him, he was only thirty years old and enlightened. When a Tirthankara is born, it doesn't mean they are enlightened but will achieve that state one day in their last life. As I mentioned before, they are born with three types of knowledge, then once the fourth knowledge happens at time of diksha (renunciation), it's called Manahparyay jnan. They begin to read all the patterns of everyone's mind. When they become enlightened, called keval jnan, they know everything. I visited him when he was already enlightened. I didn't realize how high he was or that he attained enlightenment, but realized it later in my life. A master never declares they are enlightened. Only the students share it. For your knowledge, he was the first Kundalini master.

People think, "Oh, the Kundalini master was Adinath." Yes, in a way, he was, but the purely Kundalini teachings comes from the first Kundalini master Parshvanath. After his nirvana, his disciples didn't know how to preserve his main teachings and keep them safe because there was no writing system, so through the statue they added the seven hooded snakes on the top of his head. That's the symbol of the Kundalini and represents the seven chakras, wheels of energy. When you see the Parshvanath statues, they usually have thousands of hooded snakes.

Thousands of hooded snakes mean there are thousands of chakras in the body. But there are only seven main chakras. I learned the chakra system directly from him in that life, and have revealed a lot of his teachings, especially in one of my books *"Chakra Awakening: The Lost Techniques."*

A lot of teachings are hidden, unknown. If you keep asking me, I can reveal it. But if you ask, the answer will come only that much. I was a student and a disciple of the Tirthankara, but I was not a monk. To be a monk means you are living with the Tirthankara and are totally renounced. But even if you wished for it, you are in his presence. You will know what the presence of the Tirthankaras is. Their body, fragrance, and best particles of the universe. You can feel immediately that you are in a special place where people forget their enemies. The mongoose and the snakes sit together and don't bother each other. When you see the leopards, lions, and the goat and the cow. They are sitting, relaxing, and enjoying his or her presence and teachings.

Being a Tirthankara is a challenging thing. It takes trillions of lives to collect an abundance of virtues. It's not easy, but whoever is in their presence is lucky too. Sooner or later, the students who were present with the Tirthankara become enlightened. It may take a little time, but time is irrelevant. It comes. Any date you fix, it comes. It is there. Thousands of years, how it passes quickly, people don't know. It just flows, and time flows so fast you can not believe it. I couldn't believe it has already been almost 2,900 years since I used to know him in my past life and be in his presence.

Tirthankar Parshvanath taught the chakra system so when I read a book about the chakras from a researcher/scholar, I couldn't believe how distorted his teachings were. These things need to be straightened out and my personal goal is to correct the teachings as they were originally taught. Even though Jains revere Tirthankar Parshvanath, they don't know why he has a seven-headed snake on his head. They worship without knowledge; they don't know he was the creator of the chakra system. He is the only Tirthankara that has a very distinct symbol on his statue beyond the simple identification symbol as the base. It is unfortunate that it has been totally forgotten.

This precious knowledge has been scattered, but I am collecting a few things to preserve this. But, in my previous life, what I experienced, I can not say in words what it means to be in the presence of the Tirthankara. Nobody can explain it. You can only feel it. You can only realize it. Only you see it when you leave and you go to the other world. It's like having two selves that exist at the same time. One has to go to work and the other one cares for the household. Your life is divided into two. One is the presence of the Tirthankara and you want to stay there, but you have to work every day. If you are caring for your family and have a lot of responsibility, that life is distorted.

I used to think that the day would come that I would be released from these responsibilities and duties so I could be in the Tirthankaras' presence for the rest of my life. It didn't happen because I was already full of responsibility. I wish I could have been a monk at that time, but it didn't happen. It happened after many lives.

You need to be clear about a Tirthankara's presence and Arihanta's presence. As I mentioned, a Tirthankara's body is special. All the best particles of the universe are already in their little body. Can you believe you are sitting in that presence? You are sitting in the whole universe. Arihanta's presence is a bit different. An Arihanta's presence is different, their knowledge is the same, their physical presence has a special feeling, but nothing as strong or in any comparison to that of a Tirthankara. They have normal particles, not the best particles of the universe.

Even though there is no difference on soul and knowledge level between a Tirthankara and Arihanta, an Arihanta will still bow down to Tirthankara. Arihantas don't bow down to other Arihantas because they are equal. All the Arihantas, enlightened monks, and nuns at that time. They will bow down to Arihanta. Even they are enlightened with Parshvanath. They were enlightened to monks and nuns. And I use nuns purposely. Why? Because one of the sects of the Jain system don't believe that in the female body, one can achieve enlightenment. But I have seen it with my own eyes. Even the many kings asked Tirthankara Parshvanath, "Are these nuns enlightened?" And he said, "Yes, they are enlightened. They know what I know." I heard it with my own ears.

To be very clear, it takes a human body to achieve enlightenment regardless of if one is male or a female or the third gender, what they call Napunsak - they are neither male or female, biologically. If Tirthankara Parshvanath was here, he would declare, "Everyone is welcomed equally, no matter if you are LGBT. We are all the same. This body is the same body and anyone can achieve enlightenment." I promote the same. I have students who are transgender, and really are. They're not pretending. Some pretend, some are very confused, unfortunately, but there are some who are truly transgendered. I accept all as my students if they want to learn.

The body is not the question. The question is if your soul is ready to achieve that. It's unfortunate why the Digambar sect discriminates against females. It is backwards, patriarchal thinking. It is not the truth as taught by the enlightened ones. I know of women who achieved enlightenment at the very last moment, their last breath. Luckily, I have my own experience and memory from my life 2900 years ago to witness Tirthankara Parshvanath stating he had enlightened female students. Otherwise, I would've been in illusion, too, right? But I will never be in fantasy. I always respected whoever was in the female body or other body. They are all equal. And they can achieve the highest state of consciousness, called enlightenment.

To be in the presence of a Tirthankara, you can't even imagine. Luckily, I have this memory; every day, it comes to me what he used to say every day. I still hear it. I will reveal more, but someone has to ask a question.

Every question is the right question if it comes to you. If your soul is thirsty somehow, and your thirst is to be awakened, that will be the real question. It can come if you go deep into your consciousness with closed eyes. The real question will pop up, and the answer will be correct the same way. But how do you know if it comes from your mind or soul? I can tell. I can tell when a question is asked out of curiosity or entertainment and when it is sincere and comes from deep within their consciousness. I'm not here to entertain, so if I don't answer your question sometimes, it's because it isn't real. Go deeper and ask the real questions.

A SECRET ABOUT THE TIRTHANKARAS

Sadhvi Siddhali Shree had recently asked me, "What is something about the Tirthankaras that no one knows about, that is not mentioned in the scriptures?"

There are many secrets people don't know about the Tirthankaras. People only know of them through the scriptures, maybe, and their statues. That they are sitting in meditative state and if you go to Shwetambar Jain Temple, they are decorated like a king - they have a golden crown, studded with diamonds. Does a Tirthankara need that? Do they need to be decorated like that? No.

The Tirthankaras are diamonds. A secret that people don't know is that if someone touches a Tirthankara body by chance, they will feel that their body turns to gold. Can you even imagine what it would be like in their presence? Indescribable. Whoever meets a Tirthankara in a past life, will not be lost in the world of suffering. It is a matter of time, when they will awaken, and it will come.

In June 2015, a group of students and I were reciting mantras as usual. Suddenly, one of the Tirthankaras from another planet, visited via his astral body. He is one of the present twenty living Tirthankars in the entire universe. All of a sudden, I saw his huge enormous body appear right in front of us. He was sitting on the property of Siddhayatan Tirth, we were basically at his feet, while he was sitting cross-legged. He must have come from another planet where they are extremely tall. He suddenly appeared when I was talking about our greeting, "Jai Siddhatma." He heard it and loved it. All the students felt something changed in the air. Afterwards, they were laughing, crying, or going very deep into meditation. They didn't know what happened, but they knew something did. I explained to them who visited and appeared, they were humbled and honored. They felt the presence of a Tirthankara, and the one who visited was Tirthankar Vishal Swami.

The Tirthankaras are diamonds, they do not need to be decorated by them. They are the highest consciousness and their bodies are strong, beautiful and revolutionary. Absolutely amazing. They should make diamond statues of the Tirthankaras, that will be a little closer to representing who they really are. And yet, it doesn't really come close. A diamond is still a stone, the best particle of the universe is beyond that.

One girl had a deep admiration for me - I don't know why. Maybe she got fully absorbed by the presence. She was eleven years old and at the time I had trouble walking. My knees were giving me problems. So she and her mother would cook and serve me food. When they came to the place where I was staying, the other disciples were not there, so they sat and ate with me. By the end, the little girl asked, "Can we take you to our home?" I told her, "But I cannot walk." Her mom chimed in, "Please, do come, we will manage."

I went to their home and they lived very simply. They showed me their home and started taking me down to the basement. They had seven basement floors. I wondered to myself what was hidden here?

"We never brought any one or any other monk here. We don't trust them." They brought me to this thing with a cover on it. And then they removed the cover. I couldn't believe it. They had made an emerald statue of the 24th Tirthankar, Mahavira.

I was amazed, but of course, it wasn't enough to represent the reality. The emerald statue also had diamonds and sapphire and was 8 inches tall. The family seemed simple and poor on the outside, but what was hidden in their home was a big treasure.

They protected it well. No one would guess they would have such a treasure. The statue was created and passed on for several generations already. They had the idea - a Tirthankar is a diamond - but in the real sense it doesn't come close to the real Tirthankar body. Tirthankar statues don't need crowns, that's a tradition I don't support. The Tirthankar Mandiram we have at Siddhayatan Tirth is simple, no crowns, just a statue to represent their qualities. The temple has very strong energy.

When I came to the US, the little girl's father contacted me, and informed me that his daughter - then twelve - had died. She died holding the emerald statue of Tirthankar Parshvanath.

That's one of the secrets of Tirthankaras. We can never make a statue that will do their soul any justice. We can try, but that's not really the point. The real thing is when people can grasp their teachings, follow them, practice them, understand them. You must see your own potential, strive for that, work hard on yourself, do your sadhana - like all the enlightened masters of the past have done - and you will achieve that state. Maybe one day, you too, can connect with a Tirthankar. Work on yourself first.

Chapter 10 —

Monkhood and the Multiple Paths to Truth

In this chapter, we will discuss the question regarding the multiple paths to the truth. What are the benefits of becoming a monk versus being a spiritual student as a householder?

It is not necessary to become a monk to reach enlightenment. But yes, monkhood is the shortest path because it requires that you leave and renounce everything. Your non-attachment becomes a little more complete that way. Taking this path may seem easier, but it is very challenging. Nevertheless, it is a shortcut—a shortcut toward enlightenment and liberation.

Some people think escaping to the forest is the easiest path to enlightenment. You can be in a positive mood in the forest, but that doesn't mean you'll be detached. What about if you get attached to the birds, peacocks, and other animals? Or the trees? Or the flowers? No matter what it might be, it is the same thing.

Therefore, it is not a question of being in a forest over a city. The question comes down to your discipline and devotion. I teach that most people can be on the path no matter where they are—at home, at school, or even at the cinema. I've seen it where someone was watching a movie and suddenly they just disengaged and mentally went somewhere else, like in a trance, which started them on the path to awakening. This doesn't mean I am supporting the idea that watching movies all the time will lead to enlightenment, no. I am just saying that it can happen in many different ways. I have seen it.

In Jain texts, there is a statement that says, *Swalinga Siddha*, meaning that if somebody's born in the Jain path, they can achieve enlightenment. *Parlinga Siddha* means that if they are not born into the Jain religion, they can still get enlightenment. Anyone can achieve enlightenment, men, women, or others—others meaning *Napunsaka linga*, which is the particular word we use for people who are born of the third gender. They may have a different word in America when someone is not a man or woman; however, in the Indian language, we call them *Napunsak* or unique. Those of this third gender may also get enlightenment too. *Sthrilinga Siddha* is a term that confirms that the ladies can get enlightened, and *Purusaling Siddha* refers to male enlightenment.

The Jain religion says you don't have to be a monk to reach enlightenment. As a householder, if you are following the path, following the system, the Arihanta path, the path given to you by an enlightened person, that path can take you there.

Mahavira's chief disciple, Gautam Swami, one day came to his master with an important question. He wanted to know if a particular householder, Shatak Shravak—or any householder for that matter—could see that far with Avadhi Gyan.

It started with the Shravak saying, "I do see that much. I can see far." Gautam Swami said, "No, a Shravak cannot see that much. That is not possible." He was so prejudiced that only monks could have that level of knowledge. He said, "You are lying, you need to confess." And he went to Mahavira upset about how this Shravak could claim to see far and attained a higher knowledge. He approached Tirthankar Mahavira, "Can a householder see that far? Can they have Avadhi Gnan?"

"Yes, you have to go back and apologize to him." Gautam Swami accepted his mistake. He was known as the greatest scholar. Though he was widely respected, he was still down to earth and very humble.

"Oh, I didn't know. I'm so ignorant. I will go and apologize to him." And he apologized. He went there right away, and said, "It is my mistake. I am not perfect. I am not enlightened, but my master is. He said, 'Yes, you can see.'"

Even though Gautam Swami was the Chief Disciple and leader of the monks, he didn't have all the answers. He was always learning under his master.

Mahavira taught that householders can be Buddha, Arihanta or Siddha — awakened, enlightened and liberated. But in India it is an act of courage to be a monk. And everybody is trying to follow this shortcut toward liberation. But a householder can be just as committed and sincere as a monk. They may have their householder responsibilities, but they can still meditate and find that time for sadhana, the spiritual practices, because there is no absolutely correct shortcut or long path. It isn't impossible, but it is difficult.

Everyone is unique. Therefore what is a shortcut for one could be a long path for another. It all depends on their intention and what mode they are in. Are they in a positive mode, carrying all of these expectations, or are they not committed? If you are not in tune with yourself and your soul, it won't matter if you become a nun or a monk, it will never lead you toward liberation.

Liberation is there. We are already liberated. There is just a little curtain we need to remove. This curtain can be removed by householders or by monks anytime. It can happen immediately, or it can take a long time. It can happen with Shravakas/Shravikas (householders), students or monks and nuns, or anyone. It has to click with you. Once it clicks for you, that's what takes you to liberation.

THE RIGIDITY OF ONE PATH

One thing I don't understand about Jains is that they put down those who are not born into a Jain family and are following some other god. They say that is *mithya darshan*, which means wrong belief. If you bow down in front of Krishna's statue, a Rama statue, or any Buddha statue, they think you are following the wrong path. It seems like they're the most egoistic people on the earth. If they don't even consider another path, then there is no difference between Catholics and Jains. Catholics or Christians, for that matter, think the same way, that the Catholic or Christian path is the only path. But that is incorrect to say the

Catholics and Christians are following the wrong path. The Jain texts share how anyone can reach enlightenment, and how they can become Siddha, so present Jains who put down others show their ego and ignorance. Siddha means total liberation, and they can enter into moksha.

Recently one Jain Acharya (spiritual leader) posted a video about the Sthanakvasi Sect and how a different Sthanakvasi Acharya visited a non-Jain temple. He condemned the Acharya for bowing down and worshipping at the non-Jain temple and insisted you can only bow down to the Arihanta, no one and no where else. This means they don't even consider other paths as valid. But a monk's path is arduous, and monks can be in any religion. Not only Jain monks and Jain nuns are on the right path. As I previously mentioned, the Jain text still has ten percent truth, which perhaps allows them to get closer to the truth more quickly. But other religious texts also hold truth and only need to be more accurate.

I feel a lot of compassion for those Jains and Jain monks who are claiming that their path is the only way, or that other gods are not true gods. I would ask them how they feel when they go to Rama's temple? There you will find people bowing down and worshiping, and everyone is in a positive mood. They are in a very peaceful state. Are they collecting bad karma in that state? No, in fact they are more likely to be burning their karma.

The Jain system got stuck on this matter because it is thought to be not *swalinga*. Swalinga means "not from the Jain religion." They think if it is not the Sadhguru, it is not the real teacher. They wonder why you are bowing down to them. They will believe that worshiping at Rama's temple is mithya darshan or wrong vision. But this is where their thinking got stuck. What if that person is praying to Jesus at a church and they've gotten in touch with their soul? What will you think about that person? Jains will claim that it is mithya darshan because that person is bowing down to Jesus, who was not even enlightened. But that is secondary. The first thing to ask yourself is who you are? What mode are you in? Are you the type of person who is willing to go deep and touch the bottom of your being? If you are touching the bottom of your being, no matter who you are— a man or a woman, a eunuch or a third gender or a transgender —whoever you are, are you following the other religion? No, so that is secondary. First thing you have to answer is: who am I?

The reality is if you are in touch with your soul, even if you are not a monk yet, you are already monk-like. You may follow more than monks who have even taken their vows. If you are living in your soul, you are always in a better boat.

MONKHOOD FOR THE WRONG REASONS

If we look at the past, for example during Tirthankar Mahavira's time or the times before it, it seems like there were thousands of monks ready to be initiated. Yet in modern times, only a few real monks are willing and prepared. What is it about our current society? Is it karma, or is it the era?

The reason for this is that in previous centuries there were fewer distractions. There were very few avenues available for entertainment, much less digital entertainment. There was no cell phone in your hand or television in your living room. No technology to take up hours of your day.

People also had fewer necessities. During Mahavira's time, there wasn't even a clothing industry yet. Because there was not much to do, people had more spare time outside of work. Being so relaxed, some began to think that life was boring. Perhaps they watched Mahavira and felt that he had an exciting life. Maybe this is why some wanted to be a monk and live another path. But that doesn't mean they had pure desire or actual willingness. They just did it because they became allergic to boredom and didn't like it. They began to say, "Oh, this life is nothing." Perhaps some became so discontented, they began to search another path. And yet even if boredom wasn't a pure enough reason to choose monkhood–or strong enough reason to choose —at least people were searching.

But this era is different. Today everyone's hands are so busy with their digital devices that they don't even have the luxury of feeling vairagya (boredom). I say luxury because, paradoxically, it is often viragi (non-attachment) that causes people to search for something less boring and more meaningful to do with their lives. When people realize that money, pleasurable addictions, and all of their other lesser luxuries eventually bore them, then they will come. They will begin to ask questions to seek the truth.

Although not many are there yet, the time is coming when there will be many monks once again. After people become allergic to materialism, that allergy will evolve into detachment–and then many will be willing to choose a different way. Hopefully, people get bored enough that I can make the entire world monks! I'm kidding.

WHO SHOULD BECOME A MONK?

People ask me what I look for in a person interested in becoming a monk, and many have approached me with this desire. The qualities I look for in a person interested in being a monk include the following:

First, the person has to be willing to be on the path. Willingness comes first. If there is no willingness, even if they are under training, it will become something like enlisting in the military and the rigorous discipline that is required. Discipline will follow, and many people are very disciplined but don't need to become a monk. They are in monkhood. Not because they want to follow the rules like in the army, it's the same for monkhood.

Monks' rules are strict, and many people will follow even stricter rules than Tirthankaras. A Tirthankar can be flexible. For instance, someone once said, "I would like to do three days of fasting. Can I do it?"

"Yes, you can do that."

But the next day he approached and the Tirthankar said, "I don't think I can continue. Can I break my fast?"

"Yes, you can break it."

But this flexibility is typically not found in the military. An enlightened master is also flexible. They do not support forced discipline, because it creates anger/resentment in the student. When there is no room for flexibility, it becomes too strict like the military. If you have to make your bed, you have to make it. If you don't do it, you're going to get punished. But in monkhood there is no punishment of this kind because discipline is voluntary. Monkhood is chosen because you want to follow it. But how many people have this disposition? There are many who follow the rules because of self-discipline, when obedience comes from your soul only, not by force but voluntarily. The desire comes to you by itself.

Some have entered training but then never finished it. Even if I accept someone into the monk training, it isn't guaranteed they will survive. Similarly, many people take *Diksha* in India, which is a ceremony in which a guru initiates a student into their teaching, but then leave in the middle because they cannot continue to follow the difficult path.

As I mentioned before, the monks' way seems easier, but it's the most difficult. People are often just excited to be a monk, but are not ready for the self-discipline that is required. Many children or girls want to be a nun, but when the reality comes, they change their minds. Reality is different and requires more than just the ability to "follow discipline" in order to survive. It is not guaranteed that a student under training will pass. Even if a student does pass and becomes a monk, it doesn't mean they will remain a monk their whole life. It's not a guaranteed path in this life that they will survive, because of the excitement. Excitement doesn't mean you will make it through the training.

That said, even if a student might leave in the middle, I will still give them Diksha. Why? Because even if you are in monkhood only one day—I'm talking *just one day*—do you know how much karma you burn? The stages of becoming a monk and the excitement of it last for a while. During that time, they burn so much karma. Even if bad karma is on the way and a student leaves, they have at least tasted something.

Yes I can guarantee that even if a person becomes a monk and they leave, they won't be entirely drowning in the ocean of suffering. They will not get totally lost. Time will come, and they will come up for air again. But the teacher might still initiate the students' training. The monk may be in one month, two months, one year, or two years when they are on the path and away from all the sins. They are not killing or hurting anyone. They are in a positive mood and thinking good thoughts. So even if bad karma eventually comes and they think, "Oh, this is challenging, I cannot follow it"—everything still counts. Every hour in monkhood counts toward preventing you from getting lost in the world of suffering.

HOW

The Everlasting Spirituality of a Spiritual Student

PART III

Chapter 11 —

Siddha & Godhood

We talked about the Tirthankaras, and I shared my experience learning under Tirthankar Parshvanath. The next natural question is, what happens after enlightenment? What is liberation? What is moksha? And what is siddha?

Siddha is a unique word in Indian culture, especially in the shramanic tradition. Siddha literally translates to "perfected one" and is a state of *asharira*, meaning no-body. Bodiless. When you become a Tirthankar, arihanta, or an enlightened one, you are carrying your last body. This last body is our final karma. We carry a good or bad body, sick body, or healthy body, so if it is healthy and a person is leaning toward spirituality, then they can use this body to grow. It's a blessing if a person has a healthy body.

When enlightenment happens, enlightenment is like a blissful state. Even if they are in their last body, they are feeling or are having the same bliss as God has. And God, as I mentioned, is not a person. That's what I said in the beginning.

God is not only asharira (bodiless), God is also formless, which we call *nirakar*. *Akar* implies shape, and so nirakar means no shape or form. Thus Siddha is also shapeless, intangible, ethereal. And what is Siddha when their last body has come to an end? After that last breath in the body, it has to go somewhere.

As soon as the soul leaves its final body, the soul by nature is already lighter, and light things flow upward. Like a balloon filled with the lightness of air. When you release it, the balloon is going to ascend upward. Smoke also goes upward. It doesn't go downward because it is light. Like how butter or lassi will float to the top of water because it is lighter, the nature of the finer matter goes upward. Besides, the soul doesn't have any other purpose now on earth because whatever it is supposed to achieve has been achieved.

Bliss is the last thing. And bliss is always eternal. Once you reach it, it stays with you forever. It is actually with you already. It is just a matter of realizing it, experiencing it, or feeling it. We don't create bliss. Bliss is our nature. We just don't know that it was always with us. It is just our illusion that prevents us from accessing it. Some think that this is because our blockages are blocking it. Not true. Feel it. Even if it's just the feeling of it, once in a while, that's what I am talking about. Brahma means God, and it is often said this bliss is like a Brahmananda Sahodara, which means "born of the same womb as the Absolute," or brother of God. Bliss is the very nature of God, the nature of the enlightened soul.

Bliss is an exciting thing. Because it is eternal, it is always in you. It is not like when you are happy. The nature of happiness stays the same. Bliss changes in every moment. Every moment is new, exciting, and never dull. I have seen wealthy people who are terribly bored. Money doesn't mean anything to them anymore and they want to find something new.

In Siddha-hood, the soul goes upward. Where does it go? That's what people need to know. This whole universe is divided into two. One half is called *loka*, and the other is called *aloka*, but these both make up one universe.

The universe has two main types of particles: dharmastikaya and adharmastikaya. Dharmastikaya is any matter that helps us move, just as water helps a fish to move. If there is no water, a fish doesn't move. While dharmastikaya is the matter, or material, that helps us to move—its opposite, *adharmastikaya*, allows us to stop. Because of adharmastikaya, which means "lack of matter," whenever we want to stop, we can control it. Whenever we want to walk, we can walk. When we want to stop, we stop. The whole universe is filled with these two things to allow us to do these two actions. We don't think about it, but that is how it is scientifically possible.

When the soul is free, because karma is the heaviest thing, it becomes weightless, karmaless. There are eight main karmas, and when a soul is entirely free from each one of these, they are empty. Now one hundred percent free, the now liberated and weightless soul begins to move upward, and it keeps going until *aloka* (non-cosmos) is touched—the highest part. That's what we call that space where they cannot proceed further. The liberated soul stops where dharmastikaya ends, because it is unable to move further beyond that point.

Where the soul cannot proceed further is called *Siddhaloka*, or the place where God lives. This is where all free souls go. They are in bliss like God is always in bliss. So siddha is an entirely free soul. We call it liberation. We call it nirvana. We call it parinirvana. We call it mukthi. We call it moksha, which means you are released and liberated.

People often don't understand what you are liberated from. The best way to know this is by understanding the concept of karma. Karma makes you suffer, keeping you trapped in this suffering world. Once karma is free, all your inner bodies—our astral, fire, and karmic bodies—are empty. There is no information in it. Everything is deleted. The soul becomes free, and it begins to go upward. Siddha is a free soul because a siddha is karmaless. Nothing else, just the purest soul. There is no heaviness and no karma with it.

So siddha is a unique concept. But it is not a concept. It is a reality. God is the purest one, and siddha means God. God is always totally free. And if somebody wants to taste authentic freedom, they must achieve the Siddha-hood.

Siddha-hood is very difficult to achieve. Of the eight karmas, vedaniya karma, stays until the last breath. It means you feel sukha and dukha. You feel pleasant and unpleasant. You feel comfortable and uncomfortable. You feel pain and suffering and happiness. That's the result of karma.

Siddhas are nameless. No identity. I wrote one poem one time while I was sitting in this siddha mode.

Chalo chale aba par gagan se.
Jahan basera bin tan man se.

Let's go cross to this all-space
Where you reside, your home, there is no body, there is no mind.
There is just your soul.

That is called Siddhaloka.

Total freedom cannot be achieved unless you become siddha. Sometimes fear comes up in meditation because you're losing your identity, and your thoughts. You're disconnecting from these things.

When a soul becomes liberated, does it still retain its individuality or fully merge with the ocean? That is the beauty of Siddhaloka. Siddhaloka doesn't take your individuality away. All siddhas are individuals, even though they are nameless. Their existence remains individual. Even if they become siddha, they merge with God. Even if they blend into bliss, their existence remains the same, no matter what. The light may be the same in the big halls, but there is one candle. You may have 100 candles, 1,000 candles, and 100,000 candles. Light merges with the light, but the candle's existence remains separate. In the Siddha-hood, Siddha is one and siddha is many.

In the Namokar Mantra, we chant "Namo Siddhaanam," which means "I bow to God." But the way it is written in Sanskrit, is in the plural. Siddhaanam. I bow to siddhas. By language it shows, we bow to God, siddhas, which is plural. God is not one. God is made up of individual free souls, like infinite drops make up an ocean. Similarly, with God, there is one but made up of many. Each drop is individual and a part of the ocean. Therefore, the bliss is enjoyed by every individual siddha, separately.

According to the different religions, God is believed to be a single entity, high in the sky, all powerful, living in Heaven and like a King. There is a misconception of God. The truth is, God is not one individual, but made up of many free souls. There is no one soul "directing" this world or universe. In prayer, most pray to one God. In the Samanic tradition, when you pray or surrender to siddha, you're surrendering to an infinite number of free God-souls. If one can change their view of God from single to plural, more souls have the possibility to help them.

Just say "Namo Siddhaanam," and all siddhas, at once, can help you. That's a mantra. It's a prayer in itself. But some say you cannot pray to or communicate with siddhas because they don't have a body. So how does that work?

Siddhas, or liberated souls, no longer have that instrument left because they have been freed. And this is what people don't understand. If you are talking to God, you're talking to a person. And a person has a body. But God doesn't have a body. God is nirakar, shapeless, intangible, and formless. How will you communicate then with something that is formless? You can be *in tune* with God. Like the sun is shining, you are sitting under the sun and feeling it. Similarly, when you are in tune with siddha, that is called prayer.

You have to be in tune with siddha. Siddha will not tell you anything just like the sun will not tell you anything or even do anything for you. But you are under the sunshine. It is not that you will say words. God doesn't need your words, but you can tune into the words and be in tune with the siddha.

Tuning in is different from communicating. Communication is a verbal and physical thing, but siddha is neither of those. It is pure soul. So you instead can be in tune with them and sit under them. Because Siddhaloka is at the top, you are already sitting under them.

That is the real prayer. An infinite siddha, an infinite soul, will help you. Do you have to lose yourself to gain the whole God? That's what it is. You have to lose yourself. You have to just be dead from everywhere. Not dead physically. I'm talking about when you lose yourself mentally; it means you don't know where your body is. It's like you just forget about it. It is dropped from you. And that's how and where you will realize where God or Siddhas are. In realization.

Realization is a prayer that doesn't need words. People satisfy themselves because they are feeling pain inside, and they want to ask God with words to give something else because they think God will help them, right? But they are very selfish people. Instead of putting in the effort, they take the easy way and want God to take care of everything. But when you forget your existence and are in tune with siddhas, you realize that all you need is inside of you.

Chapter 12 —

The Nature of Soul

What is the nature of the soul?

I've described the soul as shapeless and formless, but have not touched too much on the soul's nature. In Sanskrit, we call the soul *atma*. In Prakrit, it is called *aayaa*. I was reading a Jain text called *Thanang Sutra* or *Sthanang Sutra* and noticed that the first phrase in the first chapter is "ege aayaa." Ege aayaa means "soul is one." Because there are infinite souls, you may ask how the soul is one? Soul is one because the nature of the soul is always the same. No matter what and where that soul is born, be it animal or human or any living creature. Soul will always be there and it always will be the same.

SOUL IS ALIVE

The very true nature of the soul is aliveness. Why? Because if there is no aliveness, there is no pain. You have to understand there are two kinds of eternal things in the universe—one is soul and the other is matter. Matter doesn't have any feelings or aliveness. Where there is no aliveness, there is no soul. Like when you handle a stone or a rock, they do not feel this because they are not living. Non-living matter is called *asamvedan*. But where there is an aliveness, there is a feeling, it is called *samvedan*. And aliveness is the primary nature of the soul.

Where there is aliveness, there is a soul. Anything that moves, anything that grows, or sprouts—all of these plants and trees have souls. All little creatures, bugs, and even algae. If they grow, they are alive.

The true nature of the soul is a knowing power. Where there is a known power, there is a soul. This nature of aliveness, of knowingness, is everywhere. No matter where the person or creature is, there is a knowingness to them.

SOUL IS BLISS

The other nature of the soul is bliss. Bliss is the very true nature of the soul. Even though we are in a human body, we are not liberated yet, but we can still feel our natural bliss. However for most people, this bliss is covered by layers of ignorance, illusion, and karma, so they cannot feel it. But how, if bliss is your true nature, would you not be able to feel it? No matter where you were or what was happening, how could you not enjoy it?

I'm going to give an example. Suppose there is a drought and there's nothing left to eat anywhere. The children are starving, the adults are starving, and even the animals are starving. Then one day someone brings to that family a delicious rice pudding with almonds and saffron that was prepared beautifully. But the person giving it says to the mother that only she can eat it, nobody else.

The whole family is now sitting there at the table with the bowl of rice pudding before them. The children are starving and look like skeletons. The woman's husband is sitting there also and he too wants to take it and eat it right away because he is starving. Now the only condition is that the mother alone can eat it. Even though she too is starving, do you think she could enjoy that pudding? No, because the situation is different and her ability to taste the nature of the pudding is hampered. The nature of the soul is like that. It depends on the situation and the body you have. If you have a body full of bacteria and sickness, it is like it is totally dark. The enjoying power is gone. To be on that kind of hellish planet where it's dark and you cannot enjoy anything is miserable. Bliss may be there but your ability to taste and savor it will depend on how many layers you have around you. That's why I always encourage people to purify the body. If you don't have a strong, healthy body it is difficult to experience bliss.

Sometimes God (Brahman) is referred to in Sanskrit as *satchitananda*. Let's break down that word, sat-chit-ananda. There are three words. Sat, chit and ananda. Sat means eternal, true; chit means aliveness; ananda means bliss. That is the true nature of the soul, sat-chit-ananda. If somebody asks you, "Who are you?" You can say, I'm Satchitananda. That is not only God's true nature, but your own too.

Although this bliss and vitality are the true nature of the soul, as said before there are countless things that can block us from our truest selves. There can be a lot of layers causing a lot of darkness. These can be layers of ignorance, layers of illusion, layers of pain, and layers of suffering. This is what we call vedaniya karma, where you cannot enjoy your own natural state of bliss - you're in constant pleasure or pain.

Once bliss is achieved, it is infinite, it never ends, and bliss is amazing. Why does the blissful soul never get bored? Because bliss is always new bliss. In each moment, there is a new bliss—in each moment, it's coming. The atma is always new. That is the fundamental nature of the soul. It never gets old. It's always new, newer, and newest every moment. It never dies.

This is how we begin to understand the fundamental nature of the soul. If we're going to search for it, our search must be made in the right way so that our discovery can be made in the right way. Not through Google. If you search for it through Google, you're never going to find the real nature of the soul. You have to search the right way. AI, artificial intelligence, can't help you, either.

SOUL IS INDIVIDUAL

All souls are the same. They have a knowing power, a vision power, bliss, aliveness, and proper conduct in an infinite way. Yet at the same time, the soul is uniquely itself. This uniqueness however is not a personality because there is no personality to the soul. But the soul is always individual. Even if they get liberated, they still are individuals—even though when they get liberated, they merge. The light merges with the light. Soul and light are the same, and knowing is the same.

That's what we say ege aayaa, that the nature of the soul is the same. So the soul is "one," but the soul will always be individual. How can both be true? Suppose thousands of kings

sit in one room, and you ask them, "Who are you?"
He says, "I'm king. Now, who are you?"
You say, "I'm king. Who are you?"
He repeats, "I'm king."
They are all kings, right, so they are all equal.

This is the same way for all souls awakened. You ask, who are you? The answer is, "I'm a soul." Names disappear. All this body disappears. Even when the body is still there because it is not the last body, they will still say the same thing as the king who says the same thing—that is, everybody is the king. They don't lose their individuality, even if they merge with the collective consciousness. Even if they merge with what God is, God is a collective consciousness, a collective soul.

The uniqueness of the soul is a blissful state, but if you've never tasted the blissful state, no matter how much I tell you, you're never going to understand it. I have a tough time explaining it. Why? It's like somebody told me that they wanted to learn how to swim, and asked if I could teach them. I would say, "Yes, I can teach you how to swim." Then I take them to the water or swimming pool, but they say, "No, I don't want to go in the water, but can you still teach me?"

How can I teach someone how to swim if they won't go into the water? I can try everything, and tell them how to move their hands and kick with their legs, but no matter how I try to explain how to swim, the person will not learn. The best way to teach someone how to swim is by having that person go into the water. You can never really know how to swim without going into the water. Similarly, no matter how much I tell you what the soul's nature is like, and what the soul's uniqueness is, people will not understand unless they experience it or realize on their own.

There is a way to realize this bliss state; you just have to close off all distractions. Shut off all these instruments that you have, your six senses, including your mind. You have to shut off all of this, and then suddenly your soul will begin to see.

SOUL IS ETERNAL

Another quality about the soul is that it is eternal; existence doesn't disappear. That's what *satta* means, eternal. Existence is in essence the English verb, to be. You don't have to be anything, just to be, be. Once you learn how to be, it means you exist. Otherwise, you cannot be. If you can be, you cannot be without existence or eternity.

And every soul will know each other too, even if they are liberated, realize they don't have a body, they don't have senses, they don't have a mind, but they still know it because knowledge is infinite. That is the uniqueness of the soul. Don't think only God knows. Every single soul has this nature. What God knows, we know too, but we are just incomplete, yet, God is complete.

HOW TO CONNECT WITH SOUL

In the meditation retreats we host at Siddhayatan, the question of how to connect with the soul often arises.

We are souls. That's our nature. How does one connect to that and live from that place instead of our human selves?

First of all, you have to understand, when you ask the question about how to connect with our soul, I ask myself, "Do we have to connect with one? We are already connected. It's who we are." Disconnection is an illusion and dilemma; we feel we have to connect with what is already there, which is already you. So why do we feel we need to connect?

I do understand the problem, however, that people are trying to express—and that is that they know there must be a soul within them, but they cannot feel it, or they simply want that "connection" (awareness) to be stronger.

You must understand that the more you try to connect with the soul, the farther it will go away. Like people try to meditate, they cannot meditate because they are *trying* to do something that is merely *being*. Where there is trying, where there is an effort, it doesn't work. To find the soul, you have to embody the soul. It is an effortless state.

THE PATH-LESS PATH TO SOUL

People tend to want a roadmap to spirituality, and that's why people sometimes become trapped. All religions make their roadmap and its followers are satisfied because they can now walk where there is a map. If there is no map, there is no way to walk.

What they don't understand is there is no map and there is no roadmap at all. There is no road. I call it a pathless path. Why do I call it a pathless path? I call it the pathless path because there is no way to go there. How are you going to go there if you are already there? You can go and connect where you are not yet—but how will you go and connect if you are already there?

It is impressive to me that the river is better at this than us. It starts from the Himalayan mountain tops after a heavy rain, but even without a map it knows exactly how to flow and reach the ocean. There is no road map, but it still reaches it. In contrast, a canal, which is a manmade river, has a roadmap. But it cannot ever get to the ocean. Why? Because it has a manmade roadmap. It is going the way it is told to and does not naturally flow. Where there is manmade anything—any map, direction, discipline, or any type of effort—it cannot connect you there. Even discipline, austerity, and our other spiritual practices cannot *take* you there. You need to be like a river, with no map and still flowing.

If somebody can flow, they will arrive at the ocean. The ocean is your ultimate goal. This means the soul is your ultimate goal, but you must learn how to flow. Where there is spiritual practice, there is resistance. When there is resistance, you cannot flow at all. Resistance blocks you from flowing. People think their mind has clarity and that this will allow them to go to the point where they are already resisting. You are blocking your path. You have just to *be*. When you are, when you don't think about it, you find it, arrive at it, and you are there. But it will slip from your hands when you try to find it. Flowing is the best way.

The main question is: do you want to flow or do you want to follow? If you want to have more guidance and follow, I suggest people follow the religions, because religion has steps. The religion has a map that says you do this or have to do that. For example, look at the Old Testament. There is a map there, and there will be resistance when there is a map. Religions have maps, and people who follow religion like having those steps to follow. However, they don't know they are an illusion. There are no steps to go to the soul. They may pray to God and beg, "Please, give me nirvana, give me this, give me that." They make demands. The more desperate they are, the deeper into the illusion they go, but the steps they take are never going to take them to enlightenment.

If you flow and burn your karma, you will get the result and outcome. But, by following religion, you will only get the result.

What do I mean by karma? It means that for you there is no choice. You have to do it. If you want to finish your hunger, you have to eat. That is karma. If you want to go somewhere, you have to walk. That is your karma. You want to make money, you have to do business, right? Create some kind of business. That is karma. It gives you the result.

Why do people not flow with their karma and instead follow religion? Religion always keeps you in illusion. You're going to only go somewhere by following religion because they have a map, which is a mapless map. You cannot take steps. They can say, "Oh, there are seven steps to be in the now, in the present moment." There is no step to enter the present moment. Just be and you are already in the present moment. People need help understanding this. They want steps, but these are actually leading them away from the soul. You may understand what I mean. Just flow, and you are already there.

Hindu Swamis have a big organization, and they have so many steps people are ready to follow them because they want to know the truth. They want to know God and the soul. People want to understand the truth of who they are. Swamis offer many steps you need to follow to meditate. You have to do these exact things, and meditation will happen. Or if you want more techniques, you have to spend money and then get initiated, and then you'll get these new steps. Each step requires investing more money, and it's truly unfair to people who don't have it.

That's why you have to follow the pathless path. Our mind is geared towards following steps, it wants structure, but the path doesn't have form or a rigid structure. If you follow guidelines, practice the spiritual teachings, and get individual guidance, you'll have that flashlight, right? So a guru is like a flashlight to your inner path that only you can find.

EFFORT CAN CREATE RESISTANCE AND BLOCK FLOW

From this experience you will grow spiritually because you let go of trying to follow steps that create tension. It's not easy to learn how to relax. It's not easy to let go, especially in a culture where you have to always be achieving new levels to feel successful. The pathless-path releases all those ideas. For most people, it's not easy to let go of religion or structure, and they don't know how to. But when you learn to flow and let go, it will happen.

We have this idea, how-to, there's a verb, there's an action. It's a how-to. We get this question all the time, how do you flow? You want to go. You want to find who you are and how to get there. Ask the river. "Hey, how are you going to get to the ocean if you don't have a map to get there." The river will laugh at you and will tell you, "I am not trying. I am enjoying my strength, enjoying my courage, enjoying my confidence, enjoying my power. I'll arrive there."

Just let go. No efforts. Efforts stop you. Steps stop you. Think about how the river flows. It has a current. It has strength. It has confidence and thinks, "I believe in myself. I have power." But that's not just what you need to do, it's how you need to *be*. Stepless steps are when you believe in yourself, your strength, and your own capabilities. When you fully believe in yourself, you have confidence. These are not steps; these are your qualities. I teach people how to reveal their qualities. Why? If your qualities are revealed and fully expressed, you are going to flow effortlessly.

LESS STEPS, MORE ENJOYMENT AND FLOW

The Hindu scripture Bhagavad Gita is a marvelous book that shares how, without any pretext, you should just *do* your karma. Don't wish for or don't expect any result. What does that mean exactly? The Gita is teaching us here to flow. When you don't expect anything, you are just enjoying it. Like the butterfly is enjoying. A bumblebee is enjoying it. Birds are enjoying themselves. White clouds enjoying being in the sky. All nature, they're enjoying it.

A serious person is never going to get associated with the soul. A person like Krishna can connect with the soul, always smiling and enjoying. You cannot find Krishna's picture even from childhood, where he should not be smiling because he was always smiling. What does his smile mean? It means you don't have resistance. Even in battle, he's smiling. On the battlefield, he's just smiling. If somebody dies, he's still smiling because that is part of nature. Whoever is born is going to die. It's the cycle of life. Why cry until you're hoarse? Why create resistance to something you cannot change? It's an opportunity to learn. It's an opportunity to connect to your soul.

The Gita shares excellent messages, but only a few Hindus

understand. Even many Swamis didn't get this from Gita. Let it flow. That's what it says in the Gita, but they still create steps, steps, steps everywhere. But steps are never going to let you flow.

In any situation, when you flow, you won't suffer. The mind brings the suffering, but when you're flowing and in the present, suffering cannot exist. Let's say you cut your finger, and it is painful, but you flow with it - you accept it - then you don't experience suffering from that pain. Pain is pain, but you don't suffer because you're not holding on, attached or identifying yourself with that pain. The mind cannot comprehend how to flow. Flowing belongs to the soul. It is ever-present.

So my advice is to flow instead of follow. I will suggest that you don't follow me. If you follow me, you might create many things inside of you. Steps. Maybe I speak according to different situations and questions, but it doesn't mean I am giving you steps. Stepless steps are the best way. Learn how to flow, learn from the river, learn from clouds, learn from rain, learn from nature. They all flow.

I often get requests from students to provide more structure to my teachings to follow it. Step 1. Step 2. Step 3. The teachings don't work that way because everyone is different. The stepless path is unstructured, so to even begin, you have to be willing to go without structure. It makes spirituality an adventure.

Enjoy right where you are and you will never be bored. And I guarantee if you are bored, desperate, or sad, you won't blossom. You blossom because you flow no matter if it rains, no matter if it storms, no matter if it snows. No matter if hard times come your way. When you don't stop flowing, you blossom.

Flow. Just let go, and when you let go, you are there. It is so simple, but it's deep, right? It is so deep. Even when you have to communicate, there's an effort in that, but I do this because I wish to uplift other people and help awaken other souls. I share these stories to help guide students, and I live my life as an example of how to flow continuously in your life. Flowing is in your hands.

Chapter 13 —

Waking Up and Enlightenment in Everyday Life

Previously, we discussed the nature of the soul and how every single pore in your body can see, hear, and taste. That is part of the uniqueness of the soul. You can only understand if you go through it. I also mentioned that soul awakening happens naturally, but there are blockages. There are six senses blocking it because they bring a lot of stuff around the soul. Unfortunately, all our senses are open to the outside. They're outsiders. They're not "inside," and I can prove it.

HOW SENSES INVITE KARMA

Your eyes see outside yourself, and whatever is around you the eye brings in. That is the way we collect all this karma. Whatever is outside is visible to the eyes, and that's how we collect either raga or dvesha (attachment or hatred particles). As soon as we see any person or anything, either we like it or dislike it, right? If there are no eyes, there is no disliking or liking through vision.

All our senses are mostly geared toward the outside all day every day, and through this the soul begins to become covered by karmic particles. Consider our sense of smell. Can you imagine if our nose could only smell what's inside our bodies? It's the same thing with your ears. They don't hear what is going on inside, but they listen to what happens outside.

Taste is the same. It's outside and tastes whatever we bring in from the outside into our body. We can get addicted due to our sense of taste which separates us from our spirit. Even if we are not addicted, we are often too involved and attached to this sense. Cravings, desires, it's endless.

Your sense of touch, it's the same. Without the touch sense, we cannot feel what is hard, what is cold, which is light, which is heavy, which is rough, which is delicate—there are so many opportunities to get distracted and tied to the body.

Our mind is the sixth sense that is always wandering around the whole world. The mind can reach everywhere, even where there is no sun. The sun is the ultimate light source, but even if it cannot reach every corner of the planet, the mind can go everywhere.

CLOSING OUR SENSES

It is difficult for the soul to become awake until the mind and all of these senses are fully closed. That's why the soul doesn't wake up, because of all of our senses, which I call idiots anyways.

Why do I call them idiots? Because they're always bringing in what's outside, meaningless things, and our poor soul gets trapped by these blockages and all karmic particles.

We have to learn how to detach from our senses and there are many ways to close them off. It happened in India when a very old lady named Bhuri Bai, became very popular, despite being uneducated. She couldn't write or read and she got married when she was a teenager. Then suddenly, her husband died in an accident, and because she loved him so much, her grief destroyed her desire to eat and drink. Even when she tried, she couldn't put anything in her body. People pleaded with her, "Eat, eat. Otherwise, you won't survive." Bhuri Bai could not bring herself to eat. She felt she had nothing to live for now that the love of her life was gone.

She closed all of her senses, and she lived without food for years and years until she died. It was shocking. People think they cannot survive without food, but you can survive if you close off all of your senses. She had shut off all of her senses one hundred percent.

Once her senses were fully shut off, her soul could awaken. Now the soul has no choice but to wake up as the senses are no longer taking in karma, which creates fewer chances to block the soul's light. Despite the tragedy in her life, Bhuri Bai could awaken before she died, and people worshiped her for her ability to shut off her senses for so long.

BURNING KARMA BEYOND THE SENSES

Waking up your soul can happen in other ways as well. Look at Mahavira for example. When he began the spiritual path, 26 lives before he became a Tirthankar, his name was Nayasar. Nayasar was a laborer caring for cattle. He was uneducated but he had a unique quality of unwavering compassion and generosity. He learned that Atithi Devo Bhava taught that you should treat any guest you host like you would the divine. If you have food to eat, you should give some of it to someone else first. Nayasar followed this advice for the rest of his life.

When he was still a young man, all of his other companions were eating their lunch, and he sat down under a tree and waited. While his companion ate, he waited for someone to come by so he could share his lunch with them. "I will not eat until I can give," he said.

At first, he couldn't find anyone to share with, but as he was resting, he suddenly saw a group of monks who had lost their way in the forest. The day was hot, and the monks had been lost for quite some time and were very hungry. Nayasar was so happy to see them and he invited them to sit under the tree and rest and said, "You seem like you're starving and thirsty."

"Yes, we are," said the monks, "and we didn't know how to get out of the forest."

"Here, please take this food, I have already prepared it a special way, it is yours." Feeding these hungry monks his lunch made his heart fill with joy and happiness.

After that, he guided them out of the forest, but while he was walking with them, he felt a stirring inside. The soul wanted to wake up, saying, "We don't have any time. It can happen at any moment."

Fast forward to his future and last life Mahavira used to warn, "Don't waste even one kind of moment because you never know the next moment may be your awakening moment."

After the monks ate and while walking with him they asked, "Do you do any spiritual practices?"

"I have no idea how. I am not educated. I only know to give someone food before I eat. That is the only tradition I follow, nothing else."

The monk said, "No, you should sit and meditate. Here is a mantra for you to practice too."

Following their ideas about spirituality, later he came back to sit under the tree, he began to follow their advice. He didn't know that it was his last day of life. Later that evening, he had to cross a river with all his cattle in the dark. He knew how to swim, but the area had flooded and the river was rushing with a strong current. The flooding had caused many tree branches to fall into the river, and the fallen limbs were sharp.

As Nayasar crossed the river, one of the branches pierced his chest through the heart. He struggled with the branch but couldn't remove it. He couldn't believe his life was ending and he wondered if it meant anything. As this was happening, he remembered the mantra the monks taught him, "Arihantaanam," which is a powerful mantra in the Jain tradition. Fading fast, he couldn't remember the whole word, but he remembered the ending and whispered, "Taanam."

"Taanam, Taanam," he kept repeating in those last moments of his life. And by saying that, he went to Saudharmic Heaven, which is a higher heaven. This happened because his soul was awakening right there during his last moments. He had filled up his life with happiness and joy, and not only that, but it was his last day, and he was in very high thinking.

He thought that when he was dying, "I wasted my whole life. I didn't know what spiritual practices were except for giving food." Altogether, it shocked him that by the end of the last breath, his soul and his pores began to fill up with joy and happiness. He burned enough karma to begin his spiritual journey.

BURNING KARMA THROUGH WAKING UP

When you go very deep into your consciousness, into your soul, your soul wakes up. And all your karma begins to break. All these tangled knots of karma begin to break so fast, but you have to be in that state where nobody can stop you because you have entered it so fully.

I like what Australians say when they wish you a happy birthday: "Happy birthday from down under." Down Under is another name for this country—and I think this is where they are wishing this greeting from. When you go fully down and deep under, you are going deep into your soul. That is the way the soul particles begin to shake. And when they shake one time, they have no choice, they have to wake up. To wake up, the soul must go fully down and deep into consciousness.

There is a meditative state we call nirgranth sampraday. *Nirgranth* means no knots, and *sampraday* means religious tradition or system. In nirgranth sampraday, they call it *panchendriya* when one has a developed mind, they collect a lot of karma and particles of karma. These particles of karma block the shining light and the soul's bliss. When they are fully closed off, *kayotsarga* happens, which means that you totally leave behind not only your senses but all sense of your body too. Are you standing? Are you sitting? Are you lying down? It means all these senses will be fully closed off. As I shared earlier, when everything is closed off, the soul has no choice but to start waking up.

Interestingly, Tirthankar Mahavira's moment of waking up was twenty-seven lives before he became a Tirthankar. A lot of people have this idea that when you wake up you might become enlightened in that same life, but Mahavir's experience shows that this spiritual journey can take multiple lives. It seems like the most important thing for a soul is the moment of waking up because that is when enlightenment is almost guaranteed. But not always so; it just takes time.

You might wonder what's happening in that process of the twenty-seven lives. Let's say a person has their moment of awakening in their first life but still has many more lives to live. Even though during their remaining lives they're still collecting karma, at the same time they're also improving and waking up even more. So the karma collected, is it strong enough to block them? Or is it just ongoing the peeling of layers? It is both. They will get a body with five senses and a developed mind and as they improve each life, as a result they collect less karma, and they have the blessing of being born human to peel those layers. I always say that a developed mind is a blessing; at the same time, an expanded mind is a curse. It is a curse because if you have a developed mind and are on the wrong path, you collect too much karma.

That was Mahavira's soul. In another life, he became a powerful king. His name was Triprishtak Vasudev and he collected hellish karma. It's amazing. Even though those awakening moments happened in a previous life, it doesn't mean that they will always continue on the spiritual path. You can still be blocked with a lot of karma and need more inspiration to wake up even more in order to reach enlightenment.

Krishna is considered a God in Indian culture, and one day some people asked him, "How many lives did you work on to get to be known as a god?" They were seeking enlightenment but didn't know where to begin.

When he asked them where they were on the journey they replied, "Oh, we just started."

"And you want results immediately?" he asked. Then he said, "Sahaj pake so mittha ho-e." Meaning, "Slow and steady wins the race." Have a lot of patience, and you can find the way.

I'm not saying that enlightenment doesn't happen in this life, it can happen. Sometimes it only takes a moment to peel off all your layers of karma. It can certainly happen suddenly, but in many people's cases, it's not that easy. You can't force enlightenment either, and people go crazy, literally, trying to.

In rare instances, for a select few it has been easier. Jain literature records that Krishna's youngest brother became a monk when he was very young. He asked his spiritual practices from the 22nd Tirthankar, Arishtanemi, or Neminath, and he permitted him. He was not even a teenager yet and was already fully bald because of his initiation ceremony.

One day he was in the cemetery doing a special sadhana during which he experienced *upasarg*, meaning a significant difficulty. His future father-in-law, Somil Brahmin, saw him and he decided to form clay around his head with embers from this cemetery. He did this out of anger because his future son-in-law, who was a prince, renounced the kingdom and his daughter, who was arranged to marry the boy, would no longer get to be a princess. He put the embers on his bald head to hurt and kill him. While in this meditative state, the young monk's head started to burn. All his senses were entirely shut off, every single pore. Even though there were burning embers on his head, and no matter how much pain it should have caused him, he was completely immersed in meditation and didn't feel it. Because his senses were entirely shut off, he remained standing in a peaceful position, *kayotsarga*. He never moved and stayed steady in his posture and sadhana—all due to closing his senses, including the mind.

What happened after a few moments? All this karma, they began to burn, one after another, one after another. He was able to burn all this karma within minutes. It is said that his soul went to the Siddhaaloka, and was liberated, before his body fell to the ground and died. We have to find that speed to burn the karma, but I'm not saying you should burn yourself of course. That was maybe his kind of karma. As I said, he had difficulty with that kind of strong karma, and maybe this needed to happen for him. Everyone has their own story and path to enlightenment and liberation. To say it's easy, that would be a lie.

With right guidance and understanding, one may be able to invite karma that is supposed to happen in a future life into the present life. Naturally, it'll be giving you the results the way they're supposed to. You cannot avoid the nikachit karma. In other words, we call it niyati, or destiny. So you cannot prevent it, it will give the result. The question is, can you handle inviting all this karma into your present life?

But, yes, you can invite this kind of "burning" early, like saying "Hey, I am ready, can you give me the result now? I don't want to wait for ten lives to pass. Can you come now?" But to invite them is a complicated process. Gaj Sukumal, the young monk, was able to invite millions of nikachit karma, which he was able to not only invite but also burn through within minutes. But as I said before, these instances are rare.

Fasting is another way to quickly burn through karma. If you cannot do it for very long, just do it once here and there. Fasting is like inviting karma and saying, "Hey, I am ready." Sometimes when many people fast, their body experiences pain that goes beyond hunger. What does this mean? This pain could be coming from a hundred lives later in the future, but you are getting it now. This is called an invitation. You can invite them, and when you invite them, they can burn. But you cannot control when this occurs. This is one reason among many why enlightenment is not predictable.

THE UNPREDICTABILITY OF ENLIGHTENMENT

Everything else is predictable except enlightenment. Because enlightenment, even God cannot predict.

Enlightenment is possible, not guaranteed, in the same life if we start to invite karma. But if your body doesn't permit you to invite it, then don't. Forcing karma invitation, when your body is not strong and healthy, is similar to committing suicide because of how much harm it can cause if your body isn't ready to handle it. Many people will force themselves to fast, but the body can't endure it. The human body is the best instrument to burn karma, and we cannot destroy it. That's why I suggest that committing suicide is the biggest sin because with that body you have the best chance at removing karma but you destroy it because you're trying to force things.

Invite the karma according to your power. Then if enlightenment doesn't happen in this life, it can happen in the next life. But it is going to happen. Keep inviting. Nikachit karma will give their results, but if you request them, you can get results immediately. And you are liberated right away, right? In fact sometimes people ask me, what is *mukti* (meaning liberation)? I tell them that liberation from the body is not liberation. Karma mukti means to liberate oneself from karma. When a soul is totally free of karma, then it is liberated.

You can find the way, just be careful what you wish for.

LIFE AFTER ENLIGHTENMENT

People have misconceptions about enlightenment. They think after enlightenment they just sit in the Himalayas and meditate for the rest of their lives. No, that's not what happens. When Tirthankaras become enlightened, they don't just sit in a meditative state for twenty-four hours. In some ways they do, but I will explain why this is both true and untrue simultaneously.

The Tirthankar, an extraordinary-bodied enlightened person, is always in a meditative state—even if they are working, talking, delivering a lecture. Many people, especially new-age people, have a misconception about enlightenment. They believe that after someone achieves enlightenment, they don't do anything. But there is always work to do. People always, "If you are enlightened, how do you spend the rest of your time?" I jokingly share.

"Do you want to know the secret of an enlightened master? One behavior I do is when I wake up I pinch myself to see if I am alive." And then they laugh. Now in Hindu culture, it's believed that the first thing you should do in the morning is look at your hands for good luck. So why do I touch my hands instead of looking at them? To make sure I'm still here, first of all, because you actually feel them when you use touch. Even more importantly, really amazing things happen when you tell your body, this body which carries us through this life, that it has to do something—you have to stretch, you have to teach, you have to walk and talk. If you don't do that, you are not sharing what you're supposed to share with the people now that you're enlightened.

WHAT DOES AN ENLIGHTENED PERSON LOOK LIKE

Students asked Bodhidharma, who is considered to be the founder of Zen Buddhism in China, "What do you do after enlightenment?" He responded, "Laugh and laugh."

Another monk in China, Lin Chi, responded to the same question at another time in history, "What do I do? I just go to the well, drag the water, cut the wood with the ax, cook the food, and eat."

"We understand those are daily chores," they countered, "but what do you do after enlightenment?"

Lin Chi repeated, "I go to the well, drag the water, cut the wood, cook the food, and eat."

These daily activities only stop once the body is gone. Enlightened people still have daily activities that will always remain. If you just sit down all the time, the remaining years of this body will be ruined and unhealthy. A healthy sign of an enlightened person is that they are always active.

But this does not mean that enlightened people seek extreme adventure. They are not driving the best cars, jumping out of planes, or seeking wild thrills. For example, Jesus also didn't seek risky adventure; he was wise enough. But he got caught in the area by the people who didn't like him or his teachings and were humbly telling him to leave. However, Jesus was stubborn, which helps us see that stubbornness and lack of vision can take your life away.

But enlightened people don't do those kinds of things that make them noticeable. They do ordinary things that everyday people are doing. They're not trying to be famous or collect followers. Instead, they are active physically by humbly doing daily activities and chores like everyone else. I've seen many people who claim that they are enlightened and will jump from the sky. That's risk-taking that can end their life. If someone claims to be enlightened, they will not do those things.

Enlightened individuals will never stop their daily activities. They will still eat, drink water, and do all the activities that other people do. And laugh. If you are enlightened, you can still be filled with humor and joy. Don't be serious like Buddha or Mahavira. Did you see them laughing? I think Krishna was more enlightened in that aspect. He's always laughing, right? In

Hinduism, they believe that someone who is laughing cannot be an enlightened one. But why? Happiness is the natural way of the body, and you laugh when you're happy.

If you are walking, walk happily. If you are eating, eat happily. If you are listening to some kind of talk, listen happily. If you are talking to someone, talk happily. What's wrong with that? That is enlightenment.

Sometimes I laugh when people forget that even kings and queens still have to keep up their hygiene. Some are amazed that even enlightened people have to use the bathroom. Not only are enlightened people normal, but they can find humor in instances like these where they discover those who think they are not normal.

The only difference is my brain is not your brain. Your brain is like a processing machine that is always on, while an enlightened person has learned to go beyond the brain. But your soul, your inner knowing, is the only difference—and that difference lies in self-realization. Maybe the ordinary person knows they are not self-realized, while the enlightened person knows they have a big inner mine of diamonds. Ordinary people, even if they have those same diamonds, they don't know it.

That is the only significant difference. The body's needs remain the same; it is the inner knowing that makes the difference. And inner knowing is a realization.

THE MISCONCEPTION OF ESCAPE

Sometimes those who want to be on a spiritual path and take a solemn step feel like they have to run away to the forest and escape the world. Renouncing the world isn't necessary, and the idea that you must do so and leave everyday life in order to become spiritual is false. Here I am and there you will be—living a spiritual life while still in the world.

That mindset is like a fish swimming around in water, but who is still thinking, "Oh, I am so thirsty." And I want to say, "Hey, don't you live in the water? How come you think you are thirsty? Don't you realize that the exact thing you need is already all around you?"

But people who try to escape to the forest or mountain, have this idea that they will be peaceful there. "I will be alone, and nobody will disturb me." Actually there can be *more* disturbance there. There are wild animals, and there are birds, and there are so many challenges in the forest, right? Do you think that one little animal can harm your whole body? They try to imitate Shiva and Mahavira, but no, they go to the forest. That's the way they think they'll get their enlightenment. They're wrong.

Jesus could have escaped to reach his own enlightenment. But didn't want to run and wanted to stay amongst the people. And it is very well-known that the Buddha became awakened while sitting under a tree in his village. He was not in the forest, but under that Banyan tree right there in public. People gave him food, and offered him rice pudding---and that is where he awakened. However before that moment, he too tried to succeed but went into the forest. Awakened doesn't mean enlightened.

Mahavira tried for twelve and a half years to reach enlightenment in the forest, but nothing happened. Then he thought that he should go somewhere where there is more torture that would help him burn his karma. And he went there deliberately, and he must have been a very stubborn person. Sometimes, I wonder about his choices, but it doesn't mean I am making fun of Mahavira. I'm talking about his karma being so dense and heavy that he wanted to break away from it no matter what it took. He was willing to do anything to burn his karma. It took him 12 and a half years of intense sadhana and torture.

He went into more difficult areas where the people did indeed beat and torture him. They were so cruel. They didn't know who he was. They didn't know that he was once a prince. To them, he was a crazy man.

He was also naked, and deliberately went to areas where mosquitoes bit his body and tortured him until his body was bloody. But Mahavira wanted to test himself to see if he could maintain his meditative state. And he did. Not everybody can be like Mahavira, and that's why he is considered the great and one of the bravest people on the earth. *Mahavira* means the most courageous person. Mahavira did burn his karma, but not in the forest. He went everywhere. He went to the villages, and he went to the town. He went everywhere and became enlightened, but it took him twelve and a half years.

Today I talk with many people who believe, "Oh, if we go to the forest and the Himalayas, by the grace of Shiva or by God's grace, we will get enlightenment there." The misconception of having to go to the forest or the Himalayas to get enlightened there is merely an escape. And escaping doesn't lead you to soul's enlightenment.

All of the other Tirthankaras didn't escape either. They did renounce the kingdom and wanted it to be very different, to be away from the people, but they still avoided taking up permanent residence in the forest. Their idea was to live without people for a while so that they can meditate and realize themselves a little more. That was not an escape. Escape is when you are running away from people permanently.

That idea that you can get away from everything that bothers you and you will be okay there in the forest is a myth. Birds will bother you, and animals will bother you. Your past memories or trauma will hurt you. Wild animals will bother you more than people. And, do you know what you will think about? The cuckoo bird that always talks and sings. In the beginning, it will be a very soothing sound. But it talks often and all the time and can definitely be a disturbance. You'll think, "This cuckoo is disturbing my meditation. It's driving me cuckoo!" Eventually everything begins to bother you, no matter where you are.

You don't need to go anywhere to achieve enlightenment. If enlightenment needs you to go to a place, go inside yourself. Inward. That is not an escape. That is called entrance. You are entering enlightenment if you enter inside of yourself. And what is hidden inside here? Nothing is hidden outside. Everything is hidden there. Just enter there, no matter where you live. Even amongst all the people that surround you, you can be alone. You can actually be with people or with no one; but if you are inside here, your soul's center, you are with everything.

Enlightenment is everything. Nothing is better than bliss. You can see beauty all around you. Enjoy it. But no matter where you go, go to the real place. The real place is right there. Enter inside your consciousness, your soul. And everything will be open there.

Then finally you will be released from all your misconceptions. You will no longer do stunts or seek adventure because inside you is the greatest adventure you have ever had. What else is left? Yes, your daily activity will remain the same. You still cut wood because you need to cook food. You still drag the water from the well because you are thirsty, right? And that's enlightenment. It's not far from you. It is in your hand, right now, right there.

Illusion won't let us see the truth. The truth of the here and now can feel very far away. And what do you have to do to access it? Just look at your heart and enter there. And when you do, you go deep into it, deeper and deeper and deeper. You reach the deepest levels of your consciousness—and that is where enlightenment is found. You don't even achieve it. It just reveals itself to you. It's so simple, but many people overcomplicate it. Enlightenment can reveal itself to us little by little, until drop by drop it fills the bucket.

Chapter 14 —

Role & Importance of Health in Spirituality

I always emphasize how important health is on the spiritual path because good health is essential for spiritual seekers. Good health is supposed to be a priority, and without it one cannot grow on the spiritual path or go as far.

Health is very important because if your body feels uncomfortable or uneasy, it means something is wrong in the physical body. And as I frequently mention, the physical body should be our top priority because it is our vehicle to grow spiritually higher.

Take for example spiritual practices like meditation. If your body is weak, you cannot sit quietly for a few minutes. I have seen people who cannot sit silently, or quietly, their legs and feet shake. Why? Because they're not feeling comfortable in their body. The comfortable feeling is a health issue.

A healthy body is imperative for spirituality. Energy moves perfectly in a healthy body. All channels are clear in the body. When channels are blocked, like the main channels, in the yogic system, ida, pingala, sushumna, it can create imbalance. Ida is the left nostril, pingala is the right nostril, and sushumna is in the backbone. If these channels are clear, and there are no blockages at least on the periphery, then you are doing good with your body.

When your channels are balanced and clear, meditation easily happens.

You can make yourself and your body healthier again. The body is under your control, it is up to you. You can make it healthy, or you can make it unhealthy. You can either eat junk food and become unhealthy, or you can eat good food and be healthy. It is a big knowledge about the food.

HEALTHY DIET

If you realize that "My body's not healthy, how can I make it healthy?" Start eating good food. Start listening to health podcasts or learn about how to better your health.

Health comes according to your own experience with food. If you know how to prepare healthy food, with good vitamins, with good protein, etc. you will nourish your body. If you don't nourish your body with healthy food, it is going to be weak forever. Parents' first role is always to give their children healthy food. A mother needs to know how to nourish their baby if they become a mother. They need to know how to raise the baby, even when they are in the womb. Babies are supposed to be healthy when it comes to entering into the womb of the mother the same day. Mother has to be in the routine of healthy eating. Good food is different from tasty food. People often want their food to taste good over being good for you. People like to put a lot of salt in their vegetables, beans, and rice. Our body doesn't need a lot of salt.

Everything carries salt and sweetness already. Adding a little bit is good for you, but it will ruin your health if it's too much. The best thing is to raise the baby with very minimum salt and minimum sugar, not to give the whole glass of the original apple juice to the baby. People love sugar, too much of it.

These days there is stem cell research and they believe through one stem cell a lot of disease will go away. What does it mean? They don't want to work hard on their own body. If your cells are not healthy, right? You make yourself healthy by eating food. Eating the right food is imperative and knowing the combinations of food.

How we combine the food is very important. You cannot say organic meat, right? Organic fruit, organic vegetables, organic beans, organic nuts. They are possible. Being vegetarian is the first step of spirituality, for non-violence reasons and health too.

For proper combinations, I suggest eating fruits by themselves. Don't mix your fruits as you eat the other meals. Have watermelon before your meal but don't eat them at the same time. Be aware of the hot and cold nature of the vegetables and fruits. This also affects.

If you don't give this physical body good and healthy food, it will be undernourished. And when it is undernourished, it will always be weak. It is better to start from baby-hood.

I suggest that you cook your own food. Once in a while it's ok to go to the restaurant, and if you're traveling you don't have much choice. When you cook your own food, you know the quality of vegetables and you know how to combine the right foods and you add your spices. There will never be a doubt in your food when you make it yourself. When you eat outside, you don't know who is preparing it, how old the vegetables are, or if the chef is angry. Everything matters when it comes to good food and quality meals.

As a tip, it's important to cook food on low flame. If someone uses the pressure cooker, they are not getting all of the nutrients in the food. For the sake of saving time, they're losing nutrients by cooking on high heat. This kills the enzymes. Any food from the pressure cooker I consider junk food, not healthy food. Once in a while it is ok, but not daily.

When a person is not healthy, they have to start putting thoughts into making themselves healthy and looking at everything. It's not easy especially if you don't have the right habits, but if you begin to care enough about your health, especially for the sake of spiritual growth, then change will happen. When you're healthier, you will feel more comfortable in your body. When you're comfortable, your body will relax, and you can go into meditation.

A lot of people suffer because of their body. Maybe there are constant headaches and migraines, maybe the hormones are imbalanced and causing issues. You have pain in the body, you have arthritis, you have bones cracking here and there, and they're painful. You cannot walk. These are the symptoms. When your body is not feeling well, you will be with your body. That means, your awareness will be with your body and not your soul.

Sleep is also important to your health. People have a lot of stress and tension so much so it even prevents them from sleeping. Turn off your electronics and disconnect so that your mind and body can relax to sleep. Besides sleep, here's a tip to remove the black circles under your eyes: drink sugarcane juice. It has to be natural, not sugar juice, or anything processed, natural sugar cane juice. This will help. Add a tiny bit of ginger and it'll be even more effective.

It's a big thing to learn how to nourish your body. And I am going to tell you that a weak, sick body will give you trouble forever. You are never going to be emotionally stable. Your mind will always be disturbed. Weak body, unhealthy body, sick body. Everything is sick; your mind and thoughts are sick, and your thoughts are negative, right? Everything connects with your physical body.

The best thing I will suggest is to focus on healthy food. It's essential because healthy food creates a lot of energy, which you need on the spiritual path.

HEALTHY MIND

Health can mean something from person to person but it encompasses every part of ourselves. Maybe someone is physically healthy but they're not healthy mentally. Even still, they must realize that the first basic thing is the physical body;

the mind can strengthen and develop later. Because if the physical body is weak, your emotional and mental health will almost always suffer. So you must first focus on healing the body.

When your channels are unblocked, you can learn or grasp very easily anything you read, one two lines, you memorize it right away. If people don't have those symptoms in their bodies, they cannot memorize it. It means you cannot get all the benefits because your body is not healthy.

A healthy body and mind will grasp things. Your mind's grasping power is very powerful with a healthy body. And when you grasp and you are reading spiritual stuff, can you believe how fast you will grasp all these spiritual talks and spiritual practices? It will be so easy for that person.

For spirituality, a healthy body is required and has a lot of benefits to the path. The benefit is nobody can trigger you. No resentment. No anger. If we hold on to things, that negative energy affects our health. There is no ego with a healthy body. A healthy body is very much needed to fight all enemies. Negative feelings are our enemies. They don't let us grow on the spiritual path. A healthy body doesn't mean what society deems as perfectly healthy – like an Olympic gymnast – it includes overall well-being, mentally, emotionally, physically and spiritually.

There is a misconception among spiritual students because they read it in the books, "I am soul. I am not this body." While the statement is true, the real soul and sense of self is beyond the body, you still have to care about the body you have. Just because you are not the body, doesn't mean you don't take care of what you have. You have to care about yourself and your body, all things require effort - not just physical effort but effort towards having a healthy body to generate more energy for your path.

START WITH THE BODY AND THE MIND WILL FOLLOW

Before any advanced learning about spirituality, get to know your body first. Be knowledgeable about your body and health and how to keep it balanced. Body first, mind second.

During the meditation retreat, when I teach that class, it's not like all the other meditation teachers, "Quiet your mind, focus on your breath." No, start with your body. Spiritual seekers realize later, and sometimes when it is too late, how important health is and how much good health creates a lot of energy. You need energy to go into meditation and in order to also grow and expand spiritually.

Energy is so important, and that comes from health. There is only one system that promotes real meditation. It's the Jain system, but they don't call it meditation. They call it kayotsarga, which means to forget your body. And if you're feeling a headache, how can you forget it? If you're feeling pain, how can you forget it? They're using the right word, but they're not doing the right thing. The most unhealthy people, you know who they are? Jains. Why? Why are they unhealthy? They're rich, they eat good food, but which is tasty food. Greasy food, rich food. In the Jain system it says you're not supposed to enhance your senses, you're supposed to control the desires, but maybe they're just not practicing that. They're not practicing fully. But the Jain system is right. Followers are following the wrong way. That's another thing. If followers follow the same system, which is described in the text, they can be very healthy and they can be full of energy. They can be very brave like Mahavira. But if they follow it. Like kayotsarga, which is very good.

Mind is not the problem. It's the body. And remember always, I don't teach about the mind first. I teach the body first.

HEAL THE BODY TO LEAVE THE BODY

When you are not with your body, you are very healthy, and that's what you need to do. What do the meditation teachers teach you, "Hey, go inside the body," right? They want you to be with the body. Be aware of it. Witness your breath and body. No, no, no. What I promote and share is to disconnect and go beyond the body, don't pay attention to it when going into meditation. When you go beyond the body in meditation, it shows you have good health. That is a symptom of healthiness. But if you cannot go beyond the body, there is sickness there, and remember I always say that a sick body cannot practice spirituality. Sickness is a big hindrance, a big blockage. An unhealthy body means that's what disease is. Dis-ease means there is no ease. When there is no ease in the body, that's it, it means you are unhealthy. Just find the balance, how you can work 24 hours. I'm talking about working 24 hours, and you are not with the body. It's possible.

Like when a person is asleep, are they with the body? That's the way we are supposed to be when we are awake. But when people are awake, they feel a headache. They feel pain, and they feel arthritis pain, they feel knee pain, and they feel joint pain. Why? They damaged the body somehow. They need help understanding how to eat, what food to eat, and how to nourish their bodies. This is a very beautiful instrument to use for spiritual growth. If this instrument is already not working well, then how can you grow spiritually? Your growth will never happen. Many people go to the temple or church; you know what they do? They cry, always crying, crying, crying. People get so mesmerized. "Oh, it's total devotion." Is it devotion? They're crying because they don't feel comfortable. Maybe they're asking God, "What did you make me?" They blame God. They don't blame themselves for damaging their body somehow. I understand babyhood/childhood is not in your hands, right? Whatever parents give to you you have to eat. But when you grow up, you must understand this physical stuff. This physical body needs to be nourished with healthy food. Your health is your responsibility.

Chapter 15 —

Non-Violence: The Path to Personal and World Peace

Nonviolence is truly the first step toward spirituality and inner peace. In this chapter, I will explain what nonviolence is, and why it's the essential step above all other steps. First, you must understand that nonviolence is not just one of many concepts, but rather the great way or *path* to live your life peacefully.

It is called *ahimsa* in Sanskrit. I often say that ahimsa promotes dharma, but many people mistakenly translate *dharma* as a religion. It is not. Dharma is a *path*, and ahimsa promotes dharma because it is the absolute path. Path to where? To entire liberation.

NON-PHYSICAL VIOLENCE

To understand the principle of nonviolence, you have to first understand violence. Many people suffer due to violence. What is violence? Is it simply a physical reaction? If somebody is hurt, like when somebody gets killed or people are harming others, that is physical.

These physical expressions of violence are more visible, but mental violence is just as dangerous. Mental violence means that nobody will find out what a person is thinking. Maybe they are thinking about killing friends, family members, relatives or close friends, or colleagues in their office. It doesn't have to necessarily be so extreme, even thinking negatively is violence. We don't know about mental violence until it escalates and becomes tangible, and then it is too late.

When activity is not visible, the principle of nonviolence belongs to the activity, to your mind. If your mind is clear, and your intention is pure, sometimes, a person gets harmed, even a physical reaction, like if somebody is in a fight, and you try to save those people. You intend to save, and someone gets killed while trying to save. The action seems very bad, but your mental activity was pure. When it is pure, then there is nonviolence. When there is no purity, there is violence.

How do we practically integrate nonviolence towards those closest to us, so this way, we're free, and they're free too? I suggest first working on being nonviolent through physical action since it is visible. Physical not only includes touch, but being watchful to not hurt or harm others with any of your senses, especially speech. You watch yourself first. You practice being aware of yourself and your level of nonviolence. Improve your intentions.

Slowly make your way through mental non-violence. This requires a higher degree of awareness because now we're dealing with the mental activities that go on and on very subtly. An action you can catch, but a mental activity, not so easily unless you have awareness. One thing that is important is to be aware of not only your violent thoughts towards others, but also yourself. What is the violence? Any lower qualities that we hold in our life, like anger, ego, negativities, jealousy, hate, emotions, whatever, you name it. Why do we have to fight with relatives, or with friends, or among the family? Because maybe, in somebody's mind, their ego is so strong, and your ego is so strong too. Ego is a blockage.

The ego prevents you from following the path because the ego will take over, or jealousy will take over. Because of jealousy, you begin to hurt another person. If there is no jealousy, why will you hurt other people? Because of jealousy, "I want to be the best. "I want to have this thing." "Why does another person have it and not me?" Jealousy begins, if another person has it, you don't. That is the way things build up inside of you, then create violent mental activities, which could potentially turn into action. You need to clear your mind from these things because they bother you. If these lower qualities pollute the mind, the mind will never feel that you need freedom or that other living beings need freedom. The mind will be fully polluted. The mind will be fully corrupted.

When you know and witness the nature of your own mind, and how difficult it is to shift your own activities from negative to positive or violence to non-violence, then you will see by yourself how little control you have over other people. You cannot change others. If it's hard to change yourself, do you think it's easy to change others? They will fight back just as your mind fights against your soul. It's all so stubborn, but nonetheless impossible to change yourself.

I consider the mind a sense, the sixth sense, and this will take over you because the activity is more than just an action, because activities are ongoing and you can be consumed for hours and hours. The action happens only once, so the action is over, but the activity continues, and that activity keeps us from following the principle of nonviolence. Mental activities collect a lot of karma.

We need to work on these lower qualities preventing us from following this greatest principle. It is better to start working on it, like anger, suppose. Anger is a lower quality. If we begin to work on our anger, the time will come when we will be liberated from this lower quality, and other people will be liberated too. If one liberates, other people begin to feel their peace and freedom. They think, "Hey, if he can become liberated, or she can be liberated, why can't I?" It motivates them. It inspires them.

When I was with Tirthankar Parshvanath, the 23rd Tirthankar and first Kundalini master, I used to think, "The day will come when I will become a monk. The day will come." When that day comes, I can join him. Even though I never joined him as a monk, I was just a simple student. Still, the mental activity was always thinking higher, so when you begin to think higher, the lower qualities automatically disappear. If you never think about higher qualities, lower qualities will take over you. Once they take over you, no matter how much you try to follow the principle of nonviolence, you cannot follow it. You cannot have it. Why? Because your mind is still polluted with those lower qualities.

PHYSICAL VIOLENCE (TOWARD ANY LIVING THING)

Nonviolence is the most significant principle. Why? Because it connects you to everyone and every living thing. Nonviolence is the natural state of the soul. Nonviolence is when you feel the same way like another person feels, or another living being. A living being, like a little bug, ant, or butterfly. In spirituality, people say oneness, the idea is there, but nonviolence helps you to feel and realize that oneness with all. Every animal, whether it's an elephant, lion, or tiger, doesn't want to die, and they don't want to get hurt, either. They are all afraid of it. Every living being doesn't want to face death before they are ready. What happens, is if you feel oneness with every single living being, the nonviolence principle will begin, but it has to go deep into your being first. Unless you realize it, like, if you don't realize people are hurting other people, are killing others, someone else stronger than you tries to attack you, and you feel the pain, suddenly, intense pain, then you realize what violence is. Otherwise, you are never going to know it.

The principle of nonviolence is to realize, to realize mentally first. If you, or any person, realize that violence always hurts, harms, and makes our lives miserable, then they will think twice and take action to prevent the violent action or thought. They will not go for it. They will maybe make it stop. They perhaps have awareness about it, that, "Hey, no, it is the same," like, "I feel pain, the other person will feel pain." Nonviolence, why I tell them it is the greatest path, is because you are giving freedom to all the living beings, not only one, all the living beings.

That's what I tell people. "Hey, start somewhere. Start somewhere to be on the absolute, greatest path." Give yourself a life of total freedom. People think, "Oh, we are living in a very free, democratic country. We are all free." But that is not freedom. Freedom is when no one is afraid of you and you are not afraid either. If somebody's scared of you, you don't live in freedom. Freedom is the same as not being scared of anyone. They are not scared of you. Step by step, you can give all living beings freedom.

If even one person decides that "I will not have pork, I will not eat pork my whole life," that means all pigs are free from you. They're never going to be afraid of you. Whenever you go near them, they will sense that you will not kill them, harm them, or hurt them. You give freedom to all pigs in the world, and in the same way, you can decide that "I'm not going to eat beef anymore." As a result, you give freedom to the cows. You give little by little, and you can expand it.

If you can expand this principle of nonviolence, one day, it will come and the realization will happen to you. You will realize "I am connected with those living beings because they have the same consciousness, they have the same soul. I feel what they feel. I feel pain, they feel pain. I feel happy, and they feel happy." Unless we give freedom, the nonviolence principle doesn't begin at all.

The first step of spirituality, in the nonviolence sense, is that you are supposed to give freedom to all living beings. If you think about it like this, it kind of penetrates the soul. It's powerful because giving freedom to others means giving freedom to ourselves. The question arises, how, right? We're all human beings. We get affected by human beings. Some people are affected by good words. Some people are affected by bad words or can't handle criticism, praise, or these things. Then, of course, there are always situations between relatives, friends, and colleagues at work, and frustration arises. There is a way, and it starts with you.

NON-VIOLENCE BEGINS WITH SELF-ANALYSIS

I recommend to people that the concept of this principle needs to be understood the correct way, the right way. This way, you can begin to work on yourself. Unless you start to work on yourself, no matter how much you follow this principle, "Oh, I am pro-nonviolence," suppose, it doesn't mean that you are a nonviolent person, because maybe you didn't purify your mind yet from this pollution. The biggest pollution in the mind is these lower qualities. Purify it, and it will be crystal clear. Then your mind will never bother you. You will never be tempted to hurt someone, even mentally.

The principle of nonviolence is to be understood slowly. You have to go through all the little things. The central lower qualities we need to work on to realize our nonviolent self are known as one-word, kshaya. There are four kinds of kshaya: anger, ego, deceitfulness, and greediness. Kshayas pollute your soul ultimately. Kshaya is like a colored cloud. The clouds block the light of the soul just as the clouds in the sky can block the sun's light. How does kshaya pollute your soul? When a person is angry, the particles cover the soul with a unique dark color. The particles are so strong, and block the light, that it will not let the soul realize what reality is, what is truth. That pollution needs to be removed, and that pollution can be removed only if you want to understand what anger is. If you don't know what anger is, you keep doing it, and your soul will be polluted even more. The time has to come when you begin to analyze that anger is corrupting your soul. It is many layers upon layers, and my soul got trapped in it. When you try to analyze yourself, you will find many layers of anger.

Anger can show up in a person's life in thousands of ways. If somebody calls you a bad name, you're angry. If somebody calls you a name, you can snap or go crazy. If somebody stops you from doing something, you'll become angry. Anger can happen in over a thousand different ways. Anger is a strong pollutant.

If you want to follow the principle of nonviolence or understand it, the best way is to practice self-analysis. Every evening, you sit in your room and begin to self-analyze and reflect back on your whole day. Think about all of your thoughts and actions for the previous twelve hours. Think about your interactions with your family, your friends, and colleagues. Where did you make a mistake? Did you ever react out of jealousy, greed, ego or anger? If you begin to analyze and write down all the little errors and bigger ones you have made, or you have said bad words, or you were angry, write every little thing. Maybe it will be three or four pages full. Write it all. If you concentrate and close your eyes, then think about the whole day and when you have made a mistake. It is called analysis.

If somebody begins to analyze, that person will analyze the little things where anger sneaks into their soul. Somebody said something, and it's an attack on you. Anger attacks you, and where jealousy enters, you have to analyze. When you begin to analyze the next day, you analyze the same way, and you vow that "I will not repeat those mistakes anymore the next day," but it will be repeated, maybe not as much as if you are not aware. You're not expected to be perfect, it is a practice of awareness and it takes time. You will begin to see the open sources or areas of your life that trigger anger, ego, greed, etc. to enter into your life. If you are aware, it will be less and less. That is the way your soul begins to peel the layers of anger, layers of emotions, layers of jealousy, layers of negativities. Otherwise, it will stay there forever. Awareness is the key to freedom and overcoming and dissolving all lower qualities. Awareness.

No matter how many deep concepts you read about nonviolence, you will only be nonviolent if you work on your lower qualities. I've mentioned before that awareness is the key to waking up the soul, and realizing yourself. Self-awareness must happen before we can start to analyze. Increasing our awareness is like staring at a monster. The more you stare at it, and can see it fully, the less scary it becomes. It loses its power the more you pay attention to it. When the monster is angry, watch it. If you watch your anger intensely, and carefully, you will be surprised. Those emotions are very shy. As soon as you begin to watch them, they disappear. Emotions like anger don't have the strength to meet your eyes with theirs. They will be defeated by themselves. Do you have the power to watch them? That's what I call the principle of analyzing. It automatically will lead you towards nonviolence.

You don't have to read all of the books. The first thing is to start with yourself and analyze yourself so you can be free.

NONVIOLENCE AS NON-ACTION VS SIMPLY BEING

Nonviolence, remember, is not just a principle or a concept—it is the most extraordinary path. Sometimes I use the word "principle" because it's a common word that most people understand. They are familiar with principles. But ahimsa, or nonviolence, is in reality a state of being. Once your soul is clear from its pollution and you are in that state, you will be nonviolent automatically.

A common misconception about nonviolence is visualizing it only as a superficial concept of not hurting anyone or passivism. Maybe you think of nonviolence based on what Gandhi taught when he told his followers that, no matter how much the police attacked them, they must not react, not even to defend themselves. Sometimes non-violence can defeat evil, but not always. Many were mesmerized watching his followers' nonviolent protest as the police beat many and they still did not react. Many people got terribly hurt because they suppressed that feeling to respond. That suppression can be the worst thing. It is its own form of violence.

Nonviolence doesn't teach suppression. Nonviolence doesn't teach repression. Nonviolence doesn't teach you to hold on to those feelings inside of you. Suppressing those feelings to react is what will kill you, and thus is violence toward yourself. Suppressed emotions are silent killers. This is why I always teach people that true non-violence is vowing to never hold any of these lower qualities inside. Once this peaceful state is realized and experienced, nobody can take you away from this greatest path.

NON-VIOLENCE IS TRUE IDENTITY

Once you begin to release these lower qualities, you understand that they were an illusion—and that non-violence was never separate from who you truly are.

All babies are born, whether human or not, are born non-violent because they have never seen violence or experienced it yet. They don't have the idea to hurt, kill intentionally. They have no mind. People, animals, birds, and nature all experience violence;

it can be experienced everywhere. Even the babies in the womb feel the result of violence. The baby will be affected if the mother yells, screams, or fights. You might ask, when does this happen? The violence affects the baby when all organs are fully developed, like up to six months. So the baby can hear it and feel it because they have ears, a heartbeat, and all the organs are fully developed, so the body feels the violence. If the mother is afraid, the baby is afraid. The violence around us can affect a baby in the womb.

Even if a baby feels violence from the womb, I still consider that all babies are non-violent. They have no idea of violence yet. No wonder all babies, even the babies from the animal, are not scared of you. However, animals that have grown up will run away if they see a human. They are afraid that the human is going to kill them. A baby deer will come to you and will sit right in front of you unafraid. Even a baby snake will not bother you, he is wild, but there is no violence. Babies are babies. They are pure, and they are born pure.

When the mind gets polluted and grows in a polluted environment filled with anger and misguided mentors (including parents), it also becomes polluted. You see, the real pollution is emotions, and these hostile or negative emotions pollute the purity of the baby's mind. Violence is one of the worst types of pollution, and the baby begins to feel and experience this pollution. It is not easy to survive in this environment, but they have to, then they begin to fight it. People surrounded by violence, whether violent words, actions, or thoughts, are all they know. Violence becomes normalized. They might try to improve their body to fight it, but it's difficult because they don't know the other way.

There is another way, an easier way. Let me give you an example from the words of Patanjali Yoga Sutra. In his book he wrote, *ahimsa pratishtayam tansannidhau vairtyagah*. This means when a person is in a totally non-violent state, all the animals or people sitting around them will forget their enmity. They forget their revenge but must be in *ahimsa pratishtayam*, meaning they must be fully in a non-violent state—a state which is effortless.

NON-VIOLENCE IS EFFORTLESS

Back when I was a yogi around the Himalayas, lives ago, the people in India were fascinated by our existence. They would try and go find the yogis around the area because they found them mesmerizing. Yogis, for them, were considered next to God. They were extraordinary people that climbed the Himalayas and would stay far away, living in caves or sitting in silence on the mountaintop. One time I came out of my meditation to find hundreds of people surrounding me saying, "Luckily, you're alive! We were praying for you the entire time."

I was very confused and asked, "What do you mean? What happened?"

They explained, "As soon as we arrived and we were watching you there, we all saw a big tiger approach. Before we knew it, the tiger was just sitting in front of you."

They were all praying the tiger didn't attack me, but I never saw it, nor was I worried. Because I was totally in a meditative state, and typically in that state of being a tiger will never attack.

When a person is in a meditative state, they reach a state of complete non-violence. Even though they have a body, those yogis become formless. Even though they have a mind, they become mindless. Even though they have a thought, they become thoughtless. When somebody is in a mindless, body-less, thoughtless, and meditative state, they cannot be attacked. Neither humans nor animals will attack them. Why? Because they feel peace around them, and an animal only attacks when people are afraid. When humans feel fear, their nerves and blood vessels tense. The animal then feels something. Fearing this unexpected energy, it will then attack that person instinctively. But if a person remains completely peaceful, the animal doesn't sense this. Non-violence is a state of being where peace prevails.

In India it is a very ancient teaching. For example, we are taught that if you are in the forest by yourself and suddenly a furious bear comes towards you, what do you do? You pretend you are dead. You lie down on the ground and hold your breath. You do nothing and you become nothing. Even if that bear is going crazy and is sniffing around, it will eventually leave you alone. Why? Because now you are pretending you are dead, the animal will not sense anything. They will not sense fear because you know you don't have to be scared and that it will leave.

When a person is fully in a non-violent state, the Shramanic tradition calls this tansannidhau vairtyagah. Tradition says that when one Tirthankar is around, they are all around - all humans, all types of animals, even angelic beings; this is called samvasaran. Samvasaran happens when they gather around the one delivering a lecture. All kinds of animals and living beings come for this spiritual gathering, and each understands the Tirthankar's message in their own language. Tigers will understand in their language, birds will understand in their language, and humans will understand in theirs. Enmity disappears.

Because they are gathered around such an exceptional person, all kinds of extraordinary things will occur. The mongoose, the snake, the tiger, and the goat all sit and listen together. Mongooses and snakes are natural enemies from birth. These are two animals who grow up with the understanding that they need to destroy each other, but all enmity disappears when they sit around the Tirthankar, which is found in the Jain system, the oldest tradition in India, and part of the Shramanic tradition. Everyone sits peacefully and forgets that they are enemies.

Another example of non-violence comes from a story about Mahavira and a Chandakoshik snake. The snake was known to be very violent and very hostile. Still, Mahavira entered the forest and stood over the hole where the snake lived to meditate. The snake smelled Mahavira and slithered outside to see who this intruder was. Angry at his intruder, the snake bit Mahavira's toe. But instead of blood flowing from Mahavira's toe, it was nectar.

It's not scientifically proven that blood can be white; blood is usually red, right? Jains are mesmerized by this story. Here was this extraordinary person who a snake bit, and instead of bleeding blood, nectar flowed from the wound. But you have to understand that something is missing from this story. What did they miss? The missing piece is the realization of oneness, the true meaning of non-violence. When you feel connected and compassionate towards all living beings, from the ant to an elephant, you are in a state of non-violence. It is the same connection that a mother feels with her baby. Do you see how strong and rare this is?

A mother will feel a profound connection and oneness with her child, but it's not the same with another person's baby. Humans and animals have a special connection with their babies, but that doesn't translate to how they feel about each other. Real oneness is when you can feel that same connection with every living being just as a mother feels toward her child.

Can you believe that Tirthankaras feel this oneness towards all living beings like they are all their children? Thus, when they feel that way, when they are in that state, their blood becomes nectar. That's the real beauty of the story—not that Mahavira's blood turned to nectar, but that it did so because he felt complete oneness with all living beings. The snake tasted sweet nectar, not blood.

When a person is in the highest state of love, they will feel towards all living beings with this motherly love. It is no wonder all the Tirthankaras become like mothers to all living beings because when they are in that state, they cannot harm anyone. They cannot harm anyone, forget physically, even with their thoughts. How can a mother think badly about her baby? Tirthankaras operate in the purest state. When someone reaches this state, it is called *mamata* in our language. Mamata is like a mixture of love with attachment, and it is also a state of non-violence. It is like a mother's love and protection for her baby extended to all living souls.

There is another word for when someone becomes a mother to all living beings, like a Tirthankara. It's called vatsalyata. Fortunately, all Jain branches celebrate that day after Samvatsari and after the Paryushan. They celebrate all eight or ten days of Paryushan, Shwetambar and Digambar, respectively. After that, they call it vatsalyata. Vatsal day is the last day they break their eight days of fasting. *Vatsalyata* means to feel that maternal state of consciousness towards all living beings. I can guarantee you that if someone doesn't reach that state of non-violence, they cannot achieve enlightenment.

No wonder all of the Tirthankaras don't look like ordinary people. If you see their statues, they never have mustaches or beards, or hair. Why? Because they don't want to show the Tirthankaras' body to resemble anything like a man. They don't look like men at all. They are so full of love, compassion, and vatsalyata that they become more loving than mothers. As I mentioned before, they are pregnant with wisdom.

This explains why a person who improves spiritually and lives in a state of non-violence becomes like a mother. That's what non-violence is. If they can reach that state, the fundamental principle of non-violence begins. This is the deeply personal perspective of non-violence and why it's essential for our spiritual growth.

However, we all live in the real world, where many wonder if world peace is possible. World peace is possible, but only through non-violence.

NON-VIOLENCE AND WORLD PEACE

When we practice non-violence in order to make the world a better place, it is easy to understand why we shouldn't harm or kill anyone. However, we also should not harm anyone verbally with our emotions, or even mentally with our thoughts. This wider understanding of violence is known as the gross concept of non-violence.

In cases of domestic violence, people go to jail. Why? Because society rejects physical violence. But when people use abusive or offensive language, or think harmful thoughts, these are also extremely violent and also a part of the gross concept of non-violence. To be in such a pure non-violent state would be life-changing. But since the world will never be in that state, no real peace can exist.

There are only two instances when real peace is available. When a Tirthankara is born, all the violence stops, momentarily. Torture stops, war stops, and every kind of violence becomes still. All people, all living beings, are in that state of non-violence. Even if it is momentarily, this collective energy creates a wave of peace across the whole universe. Another moment when not just the world, but the entire universe stops, is when the Tirthankara enters the Siddhaloka. This is another moment of collective peace. Therefore, the world, in the real sense, is never going to be peaceful the way it is supposed to be. For the remaining era, no Tirthankaras will be born. That era of time has passed. The last one was over 2600 years ago.

Today we live in a realm where we narrowly understand what it means to be non-violent. Mainly the gross concept of not to physically hurt, harm or kill. It is how our society functions; otherwise, it would become too violent. But we need to teach our children the even deeper concepts of non-violence. If we don't, domestic violence and emotional abuse will continue to be everywhere. There will be more violent words and thoughts. If we want world peace, we need to stop this kind of unseen destruction.

If you wish to see peace on earth, and I know it can feel impossible at times, there is a powerful way to do it. First, you become totally non-violent and inspire others also. Spread the message about meditation! Why? Meditation is one of the most simple and powerful ways to bring people into a state of non-violence. If we can spread this message and help people to experience that meditative state, then peace is possible.

People have big visions, and they want to help other people. They want to help change other people. And for them, that's their non-violent mission. But at the same time, there is a deeper non-violence state of being of non-violence that needs to be realized and fully experienced.

A truth seeker should pursue the non-violence state of being, knowing that there is violence going on in the world and that they can't stop it. Many focus on world peace in the gross societal sense, but do they set aside that desired dream to pursue the simple but beautiful state of non-violence which frees *their* soul? In that aspect, I can tell you that it is better to stop thinking about changing the world. Because changing the world is not in your hands or the power to change the world. People cannot even change one person, themselves!

How many people wished for the death of a violent country's dictator? We want them to die, but they don't die. Even when millions of people have the same thoughts, they still don't die or get killed. It is like you are trying to change others; peace doesn't come from thinking about changing others. Peace comes only when you change yourself.

I guarantee if a person changes him or herself, the whole world will be peaceful for that person. Even if the world is not peaceful, it will feel peaceful to that individual. That's what you need to do. You need to change your vision, you need to change your way of thinking. And if you change yourself and you become peaceful, the whole world will be peaceful. Whatever and wherever you are, you will see the world the same way. If you are violent, even if the world is peaceful, you would still see the world as violent. But if you are non-violent, if you are a peaceful person, the whole world will be peaceful for you.

Gandhi wished for world peace since childhood. He learned about non-violence as a young boy from his mother, who was following the Jain branch, and who used to take him to a Jain nun. This is where he developed a big dream: *I hope to change the entire world.*

Initially he tried to change India, but what happened? Even though he was spreading this concept all over and it became very popular, in the end it didn't work. A division started to form in the country and millions of people were killed over the partition of Pakistan from India. Even though Gandhi garnered incredible support—with people following him blindly whether they were Muslim, Christian, or Hindu— the expression of this principle in the real sense, didn't work.

I wonder if instead of teaching this concept, he could have taught millions of his followers to regularly practice and value meditative states. I believe widespread meditation could have made India non-violent. Partition would happen or not happen, but that was not the question. If all were able to achieve and maintain this meditative state of non-violence, they would not be able to kill others no matter what happened, not even in their dreams. When this principle becomes a part of you—it's like trying to separate your blood from your body.

If you want to see a peaceful world, you must start changing only one person—yourself. Trying to change the entire world is an invitation for violence. Changing yourself is an invitation for peace.

It may sound simple, but it is one of the most challenging things to do.

Chapter 16 —

Practices of a True Student–Fasting, Celibacy, Forgiveness

With non-violence being the highest principle and path to live by, there are other practical ways to incorporate spiritual practices into their lives to help them advance on their path.

FASTING

Fasting is one of the most influential spiritual practices a person can do to burn karma. When people practice fasting, they should know what they're doing and why they're doing it.

Many people in Western countries think of fasting as a tool to lose weight or clear minds. Instead, I hope to help people know more about fasting for spiritual purposes. Yes, fasting will affect your body, but its spiritual benefits are the most important.

Most people in Indian culture are familiar with *vrata*, which is a vow to not eat on a particular day, and there are many ways to fast. Many Hindus will fast during the day, then eat in the evening. Others may fast for a whole day and then eat breakfast the next morning. In this culture, it's common for people to demand something from God during their fasting period. It's like if you go to the temple or church and you pray and demand God to give you something. That's what they're doing in India, fasting with demands to God. Fastings are mostly done by women or girls, usually on Fridays. They may feel a little better physically during their fast, but that's where it ends.

Fasting to Satisfy Your Demands Alone

Where there are demands, there is no more room for anything else. Whether you are praying or fasting, you cannot achieve anything if there are demands. If you are demanding something during a fast, you're not doing it for the right reasons. This misconception and practice of fasting to seek certain divine blessings happens in India a lot. There is an expectation that you will be rewarded for fasting. Your prayers will be answered, and your expectations will be fulfilled.

However, the right reason has no expectation. When there is no expectation of fasting, the fasting will begin to burn something. What will it burn? It will burn the infections in the body. It will burn the karmic blockages. It will burn whatever is in your body that makes you uncomfortable. That's why we say fasting means fire because it will begin to burn the toxins in your body, whether emotional toxins, mental toxins, spiritual toxins, or physical toxins. All of it will burn as long as there are no expectations.

Many people are fast thinking, "Oh, I am going to fast because my son is in prison, and if I fast, I can help get him out." When they do this, they might benefit physically over two or three days. They might think that they will fast until their son comes out. They place an expectation on fasting, but it is not supposed to be done with any expectation.

When you are fasting and close to your soul, you don't remember anything during that time—no food, not even your body. You are engaged somewhere in meditation or prayer or devotion, and time passes in total silence. You don't even realize twenty-four hours are now behind you. That is fasting.

When there is no expectation, no demands, it begins to burn your karma, and your sickness will go away. Why? Because the human body is like a big piece of machinery. It needs a rest. If you don't give any type of machinery a rest, it will overheat and it then creates a lot of problems and difficulties internally because of overuse. Give your body rest.

It is not so different from giving your body a rest through sleep. I am thrilled when people begin to give their body more rest as they start to prioritize sleep. What would happen if you didn't sleep? Can you imagine what life would be like? It would be a chaotic world. When you sleep, you are not only giving your body rest but also not eating.

Sometimes people tell me that they will dream about food when fasting. For example, they will dream about eating dessert or their favorite meal. That means they are too attached to food, which makes fasting even more difficult. In fact, this dreaming, craving mind is not very different from those who fast to get their desires met. The truth is there should never be demands about fasting.

Fasting for Physical Reasons Alone

The second misconception is that fasting is only beneficial for your body. As much as fasting helps cleanse and heal your body, it is more helpful for your soul.

It's interesting because as spiritual practitioners, we know of meditation, yoga, the chakra system, and so forth, but we don't hear or talk enough about fasting as a spiritual practice. Even when you look at different religions, most of them promote fasting in some way but they don't focus on the spiritual aspect. Why is that? Because it is a very difficult practice.

Hindus used to practice it and claim to have been doing it for thousands of years. They should be fasting for spiritual growth and burning their karma, but this doesn't mean they understand it that way. While quoting the Hindu holy book, sometimes scholars say, "A rishi or sage fasted for 84,000 years." So this means the system was in place, but their focus was on ego and competition. Their purpose of fasting should have been to attain absolute knowledge, but in reality they are doing it for an expectation. All the girls fast on Friday in India hoping, "Oh, give me a good husband." But at least they are doing something, right? They clear their body a little bit. I have not seen young boys fast, although I've witnessed men fast for a good wife.

Your soul has been roaming in the dark, sometimes for many centuries, and it wants to wake up. There are many things in the way. The biggest thing is karma. Karma is suffering. Karma is pain. Karma is an illusion. Karma is a hallucination. Karma is ignorance. Karma is when people feel anger, jealousy, hate, violence, or negativity. Karma is all of these things in one word. Karma is a dark cloud. Fasting is supposed to burn your karma, and when karma is burned your soul begins to wake up.

That's why we put the name transformation and liberation within the title of my fasting book. What is the result of fasting? Transformation and liberation. What is liberation? Being free from all of your karma.

Fasting Misconceptions

Many doctors have written books about fasting, but I wanted to write my own as they fail to touch on the real purpose of the fast. Many doctors have never experienced fasting, or perhaps only a day or two, but they need to be more knowledgeable about, and experienced with, long fasting, not just intermittent. It is how your body can begin to heal. Fasting is like a fire. It can begin to burn all your infections, diseases, and sickness, but it will take longer if somebody has a chronic disease or if that person is very old.

Another misconception about water fasting is the amount of water you should drink. For example, if somebody's doing longer fasting, they cannot drink a gallon of water during the day because it will hurt their muscles. Some people believe that because your body needs water, then you can never have too much. This is untrue. If you're not thirsty, don't drink it. If you're thirsty, drink it. Drink according to what your body needs. Many people get sick if they drink too much water. The point of fasting is to give your body rest, not make it work by digesting a lot of water.

One man came to the ashram complaining about having headaches all of the time. He did a thirty-two day water fast and said that his headaches had dissolved about 90%. Because fasting was working for him, he decided to keep going until he was 100% healed. For the first time, he was giving his body rest and allowing it to instead burn what it needed. Fasting clears all the channels within. I suggest that everyone fast once in their life.

Another misconception is that fasting works the same for everyone. The truth is that fasting is different for different people. People think there's only one type of body, and they don't understand why they can only fast for a short time when someone else can fast for a long time. I even explain why certain bodies fast a certain way and how we can't compare ourselves to others.

People should know what type of fasting is most beneficial for them and what restrictions will help them burn their karma. Only some people should practice long fasting. And if it is right for you, you must clear your body before you start by eating lighter and less acidic foods ahead of the fast. Then you will encounter fewer problems. The longer you fast, your hunger becomes quieter. For a deeper dive, read my book *Fasting: A Path for Healing, Transformation & Liberation*.

If you can do extended fasting—eight days, ten days, whatever you can do—then you will go through a lot of experiences physically, mentally, and emotionally. Everything begins to clear. As I mentioned, from the medical point of view, there is a microbiome in your gut. If they are less than almost five pounds in your body, your life is in danger. You have to keep that much. But if your microbiome is not good, you will encounter many problems while fasting. You have to have a good microbiome, or good gut bacteria. That said, I also teach those who can only fast for a short time how to start practicing safely in order to gradually extend the length. The results are magnificent. Even if you do intermittent fasting, it helps.

It is also essential to understand how to break your fast safely. Too often, people learn from YouTube or other media incorrect ways of doing so—for example, a common suggestion is eating watermelon or fruit is the best way to break their fast. I know those at other ashrams who also teach this. But what happens when someone due to certain conditions cannot tolerate breaking their fast with watermelon? General counsel like this can hurt people's bodies instead of helping them.

If you are fasting for only two or three days, then you can break your fast with watermelon and it won't negatively affect you. However, if you're fasting for longer—maybe eight days, ten days, or longer—your system has adjusted to a new way of living; your body has warmed up and slowed down in marvelously healing ways. It is almost as if it is sleeping. So cold watermelon would give it a shock, and if you break your fast that way you might undo all the good you have done for your system... and hurt, damage it. I've seen it before with stubborn fasters, they think they know better, then they're crying because they are in so much pain.

Fasting and Addiction

Fasting also helps the body and mind overcome addiction. That's the biggest thing I teach in my addiction workshop. In my experience, drugs are not the most prominent addiction. Drinking alcohol, smoking, mushrooms, hashish, other drugs or even watching pornography, these are not the biggest addictions people face.

The biggest addiction is food, and that if somebody can let go of food for a period of time, they can do everything else. This is because food is tough to drop, so whoever does it successfully is a courageous person and has shown promising mastery over the body. Fasting can help take you out of sickness and become healthy, and a healthy body can grow spiritually very quickly. In contrast, a sick body cannot grow spiritually until that sickness is gone.

Fasting is a multi-dimensional experience. In spite of the marvelous things that fasting does for your body, as I said in the beginning, these results pale in comparison to what it can do for your soul. Burning internal toxins and diseases is important, but if you fast for the right reasons, you will burn something even more important—which is your karma. And that will cause you to grow spiritually in greater ways you never imagined.

If you grow spiritually, then you will know who you are. Otherwise, you will roam around in the dark for all of your life, and this life will be wasted. It is a precious life. Use it for the right reason.

CELIBACY

Brahmacharya is a teaching that dates back to the Upanishads regarding sexual purity, marital fidelity, and chastity. For those who have taken vows, it means sexual restraint—to simply live the way you were born–alone.

Most spiritual people who have taken vows–from traditional

Buddhist monks to Mahavira's disciples–have been taught to practice celibacy. However, celibacy has come to mean suppression, and neither Mahavira or Buddha ever taught suppression. Yet most monks practice celibacy and merely suppress themselves from their desires.

There is so much suppression happening in India, among householders as well as the traditional monks, nuns, and Swamis. It is like even householders believe, "Oh, love is bad." For some reason, emotional and romantic love is a bad thing there, like a husband and wife. I can guarantee that many people in India are brainwashed into believing they should feel ashamed after making love to their spouse. They think, "Oh, we did something wrong. We sinned." They are suppressing themselves. They keep suppressing, suppressing, and Mahavira and Buddha never taught suppression.

It's the same in Christianity and Catholicism. They believe everything that happens is a sin, and they cannot eliminate it. If a traditional nun had the thought, "Oh if a man in my dream comes to me ..., " she would think it was a sin for doing so and that she was going to hell. But again, they are not promoting real celibacy, they are teaching and practicing suppression. Celibacy is in fact the wrong word.

As I mentioned at the beginning, the real word is Brahmacharya. *Brahma* means God and *Charya* means you are flowing into godhood. I like to define it as "close with God." If you're in any kind of desire, you are not close with God. Brahmacharya is not limited to sex, but actually to all desires. Clearly, suppression has nothing to do with it. Whether Catholic, Hindu, Jain, or other—many monks are celibate, but they're not Brahmachari. Their "success" has come through suppression. If a beautiful person passes by one of these monks or nuns and they are attracted to that person, it is important to acknowledge that something happened within them.

But with a true Brahmachari, hundreds of people can pass by and nothing will happen within him or her. Attraction is all mind creation–and mind creation is so pervasive in today's world. The mind is everywhere, and that is why spirituality is nowhere.

Brahmachari means no reaction, no matter who goes or passes by. No reaction at all. There are countless stories about Mahavira and Buddha sitting on the ground meditating completely unphased by what was going on around them–but they never taught about suppression. Suppression is not meditation; meditation is non-striving.

People follow spirituality for the wrong reasons and often simply imitate each other without any inner understanding. "Oh, my friend, she just got into spirituality. She's so peaceful and calm. And she's even sworn herself to celibacy now." But they don't know what their friend does all day, and even less why that friend "does it," if they even do.

This kind of spirituality becomes a competition among them. "Oh, I am going to follow too. I'm going to do this and that." But this is all for the wrong reasons. It is not coming from the inside, the heart. When truth clicks to somebody's heart, it is accurate. If it doesn't click, they will hear something from a friend, or the teachings from a teacher that has thousands of people listening, and they decide to go along with the crowd.

But when you follow the crowd, it doesn't mean you understand or deeply believe anything. Often so-called spiritual people follow the crowd with their actions, rather than freely "flowing into godhood" like true Brahmachari because of their inner knowing.

FORGIVENESS

One of the most profound questions that I get asked over and over again is about forgiveness. Students will ask me, "What does real forgiveness mean to you? What is real forgiveness?" It is an important practice for people to learn and integrate into their lives.

In Sanskrit, forgiveness is kshama. *Kshama* translates to mean "where anger is absent." If anger is present, there is no forgiveness. Forgiveness cannot co-exist with anger and must be dissolved. That's it. Then forgiveness will happen.

It is hard to forgive, though. Why? We tend to hold on to too much and it piles up. If you don't work on it, it is going to get old and older. And older things become heavier and heavier. Even old habits grow heavier with time.
Therefore, it is better to work on forgiveness as quickly as possible and as soon as possible.

It might seem like your anger is coming from others and what they do to you. We tend to avoid realizing that the anger is within us; others only trigger it. External situations may trigger it, but ultimately the anger lives inside of you. When something triggers you, you are full of rage. But if anger doesn't get triggered and just lies low simmering, that's what resentment is.

Resentment is a member of this larger family called anger. And if this whole family becomes absent, forgiveness will happen. Some other relatives or family members of anger include frustration, irritation, agitation, impatience, enmity—all of these signal that a person holds a lot of anger. Any emotion that makes you feel upset is related to anger. Even if a person is unhappy, that is anger. It's a big family!

Even the smallest bit of awareness and understanding about the origin of these emotions helps to drive them away from you. Forgiveness is impossible until anger and all of its relatives are absent from within you. Before that, it is fake. How can forgiveness be fake? People will say, "I forgive you" so easily. Unfortunately, people love this kind of fake forgiveness. Why? Because its source is the ego and not the soul.

Ego drives this kind of forgiveness because it is insincere and instead puts the other person down. It is like you are placing yourself above them when you point your finger at them and say, "I forgive you." That is not forgiveness. That is another family member of the ego. (Ego has a big family too!) When people forgive like this they are comparing themselves to you, and you are coming up smaller because they are the forgiver.

Self-Forgiveness as a State of Being

Forgiveness is not a verb, it's a noun. Just as kshama means the absence of anger, so forgiveness is a state of being. Many people mistake it for a state of doing, as in how God will forgive you or how Jesus said on the cross, "Father, forgive them. They don't know what they're doing." This describes an action, but in reality it's just a state of being.

To forgive yourself can be the most difficult of all. This is because we hold too much inside. For example, the survivors of sex trafficking somehow are rescued or they are saved. They might struggle to forgive their traffickers, but it's even harder for them to practice self-forgiveness. They carry so much resentment and shame, forgiveness is very challenging. Many people in this world, I would say the majority of people, know what they have done, but they struggle to forgive themself.

It is also challenging because there is no one else to blame. There is only you. It's easier to hide from others than to hide from yourself. You cannot hide the wrongs you've done for yourself. People know if they have killed someone or they have hurt someone. They know it, and their soul, and their life will not be clear at all unless they forgive themselves. When you begin to think about yourself and not the other, it means you are beginning to work on forgiveness — to forgive yourself.

You might wonder, "How will they forgive themselves?" There is one more essential thing that has to become absent before forgiveness can happen and it may be the most difficult—guilt. Where there is guilt, there is no forgiveness.

Imagine if somebody asked for the forgiveness of a person they harmed, and that person freely forgives them. Then the conflict is over, right? An apology was made, and forgiveness was extended. But that person who caused the harm is most likely still holding onto guilt. Guilt is a silent killer that works twenty-four hours a day, and when a person is holding it, they cannot forgive themself. If forgiveness doesn't happen, either for others or for yourself, you're never going to grow spiritually. You have to have forgiveness. You have to forgive yourself.

In the Catholic religion, they have confession, right? The priest sits inside the window curtain while somebody's confessing, "I did this crime, or I did this wrong thing." The priest may be listening, or who knows? Maybe that's why they place the curtain there. Of course I am just joking, but I do have some friends from India who are Catholic priests, whom I asked once if they always listened to confessions. He said, "Oh, to tell you the truth, we get bored listening to everything all day again and again. We nap, and then we have a penitent phrase to say. We tell them, "Oh my child, God forgives you.'" And as soon as the person hears that God forgives them, they feel released. But it is not a permanent release; it is only temporary relief, and it often comes back in a matter of days to weeks.

The Jain system is one of the few religions with a confession system that focuses on forgiving yourself. Jain monks and nuns are supposed to be trained in that, because forgiveness doesn't happen unless guilt also dissolves. Since the beginning, the Jain religion is nearly the only one with a confession system that comes with consequences for sin. They punish that person according to the crime, and during that punishment, the person has to undergo a self-analysis. I shared about self-analysis earlier.

Self-analysis is the best way to wipe out the guilt. This allows them to process their layers of guilt until they begin to see clearly. Who they are, what happened to them, and why they have had this guilt for so long. This is how, little by little, the layers of guilt begin to fall. This punishment is a process that liberates the person from their guilt and moves them into self-forgiveness. I wish the Catholics could have adopted the whole system, but they adopted only half of the process. If they had, they could have helped millions of people. Can you imagine the ripple effect? Unfortunately, they didn't want to do that. Their confessionals stop when they place forgiveness in God's name, but the guilt still remains.

Sometimes I think the Jain religion is everywhere. Why? They may call it Catholicism, but it seems like an imitation of Jainism to me. If you read the Jain system and the Catholic monks and nun system entirely, it is surprising how similar they are. Their style of dress and colors may be a little different, but much of the system is the same. They feel compassion, they feel love, they feel everything similarly. The Jain system is historically at least five thousand years old, and Catholicism is only 2,000 years old. I sometimes wonder if Jesus adopted much of the Jain system and wanted to incorporate it into his teachings, but they didn't let him. He might have tried to convert everyone to Jainism, but he couldn't do it before he died.

Once guilt is gone, forgiveness will happen, and then you can finally forget about it. Otherwise, you will always remember, and where there is remembering, there is no forgiveness. Otherwise, it continues to build and build inside of you. You realize you are carrying this burden when you try to sit in meditation and find it's difficult because you've been holding it for so long it has become like concrete.

It is better to talk about what you've done right away—let it go right away, confess it right away, share it right away, and get it out of your system so that it won't become heavy and solidify. It's like you have to stop it in its tracks. In this way, we must change how society works. Because society says you have to smile and suppress your emotions, that you can't react or fully express yourself. In a way, it's troublesome because society teaches you not to say anything. Be quiet. But now you're in pain for a long time.

Where there is suppression or repression, and someone is telling you not to be angry–you will still be angry. It's better to let them talk. This way, the anger can at least be released. The longer you hold onto anger, new anger will simply layer over the old anger, building up more and more. And as I said before, old anger does not easily go away.

Forgiveness and Old Resentments

I'll give you an idea of how old things are almost impossible to take away. I was in India one time. One family brought one little child who was around eight years old. His parents wanted to talk to me personally first. His parents shared that their son had a bad habit of eating sweet candies until his teeth started falling out. The parents told their son to stop eating so much candy otherwise, he wouldn't have any more teeth, just like Gandhi. The son didn't listen.

He said, "Next year, I am going to drop this bad habit. I am never going to eat chocolate." But the following year comes, and he says the same thing again. "Next year, I am going to break this bad habit, don't ask me this year."

The parents tried everything and took him to too many places to get help, a psychologist, and Hindus swamis. The parents came to me because they felt like my background could help him.

I took him to the garden, and we were out somewhere, and I asked him as he walked with me. "Hey, are you a strong boy?"

"Oh yeah, I am very strong."

"Look, this little plant, can you take it off?"

"Yes, I can take it." He pulled it. It was a little plant. Weeds.

Further, I went where there was a little bigger plant. I said, "Can you pull this one?"

And he said, "I can try." He put a little more strength, but he pulled it.

As we walked further, I saw a vast weed that would require a lot of strength to pull it out. "Can you pull this weed?"

"I can try," said the boy. He tried, he tried, he tried, he tried. It took him 15 minutes, but he was able to do it.

Further, there was a mighty tree. I asked the boy, "Can you pull this tree?"

He said, "I don't think so." Then he tried to climb it, he climbed on the tree, and it didn't move.

"Look," I told him. "When it was a little plant, you could pull it out. When this is bigger, you put in a little more strength. You still were able to. Third, you did. You struggled, struggled, but you still pulled it out. When it came to the tree, you could not do it. Habits are the same. When they are new habits, like a new plant, they are easy to pull out or stop. When they get older, like a tree, you cannot."

He said, "I got it, I got it, I got it." And he was so happy, "I'm going to drop my habit. I don't want my habits to get older."

The psychologist couldn't do it, right? Giving this boy a little vision helped him see how to fix his habit. He dropped everything the same day. I didn't say to drop it, but he dropped it. Why? Because he understood.

I suggest that if people really want to experience the power of forgiveness or forgive themselves, do it as soon as possible. Don't let your guilt get older. Work on it before it grows ancient and harder to remove, like a tree.

If someone harms you, don't pretend to let it go. If you secretly hold on to anger, it will build up inside of you, and then the only person you are hurting is yourself.

Practice self-analysis by examining your anger. How many people can actually sit with themselves and be willing to see? Everybody wants to change others, but never themselves. Identify and become honest about what is only poisoning you and you will begin to set yourself free!

Chapter 17 —

How To Not Get Affected by Negativity and Negative People

A common question that comes up for spiritual practitioners is how not to get affected by others, especially when they're doing their best to be calm, positive, non-violent and implement the teachings to improve themselves.

In day-to-day life, someone might criticize them, or even another's mood or negativity, affects the actual individual. So how can you become less affected by others? You are bound to be affected when you live in society. There is no way you can escape it because society taught us to live that way. If somebody calls us bad names, we get affected by it. If somebody frowns at you, you get affected by it.

Sometimes your mere existence gets affected by people because you live in a society. There is no way a person cannot be affected by it. That's why I said many times Buddha ran away from the kingdom. He thought he would not be affected by the forest. Poor guy, he spent six years, and he got bored. He ran towards the city again. Mahavira was an even worse case. He took twelve and a half years to realize it. He was standing in the forest, and he thought, "I will not be affected by it." Right? Then as soon as something happened to him, he ran to the city. In society, no matter what, if you are taking your mind with you, you will take the whole society with you no matter where you are. That's why people think, in the forest there is peace. It's not peaceful. If you are peaceful, you can be anywhere.

One man I knew of was waiting for the train and out of the blue something clicked inside of him. He realized, "Oh, my children, me, my wife, we are not real." Something happened, a realization happened to him, and he became famous. Where did it happen? At the railway station. His click didn't happen in the forest, it happened to him at the railway station. Even when you are in the crowd, you are not in the crowd. That's what you need to understand yourself. The crowd is there, but you are not in the crowd.

If you are not identified with the crowd, you are very peaceful, and nobody can affect you emotionally, physically, and mentally. There is no way. But if you are in the forest, but your mind is with the crowd, you will be affected there. Why? Little things will affect you. Why are these birds too noisy? Because that is their habit of chirping. To sing, right? Well, luckily, Buddha and Mahavira, they were very lucky there was no mockingbird in India. Otherwise, they would be annoyed in the forest. We get affected by everything because we carry our minds with us. Why are we carrying our minds? Because we are very much not settled in our bodies. If we are settled in our bodies, our minds will not carry the garbage that we are carrying. We are carrying the whole society with us. Whether we are physically in the crowd or not in the crowd, others are bound to affect you. The big realizations happen when others disappear. But it is our habit. We always cling to others. We think that we feel comfortable, and we feel at ease because the other is there; we think we're secure, and we are protected. In reality, no one can protect you.

It is your time to realize that if we are calm and peaceful and settled inside, then we cannot get affected.

When there is chaos in the mind, the body gets affected. Society works that way. Society works through the mind because we've been raised that way. If someone hurts you, and they don't say sorry, your mind is disturbed and your body gets affected - maybe your heart hurts or your blood pressure goes up. If the person says "sorry" then your mind is at peace, and your body relaxes.

When we experience that chaotic state in our minds, sometimes it gets settled down by itself. I suggest that no matter how many people are throwing garbage on you, don't be affected by it. Otherwise, we get affected by little things.

I remember... I will not give the name, but one lady was dropping me to the airport with her two children in the car. One was a little boy. He was crying all the time because she said, "Oh my baby, just get ready. We have to leave. We have to go to drop him off at the airport." And he started crying. "Why did you call me a baby?" He was two years old, not even two. He said, "I don't wear a diaper anymore." "Oh, no, my baby, I will not tell you again." "You just said I was a baby again." See how much he got affected by it? I took him to my lap and said, "Oh, I didn't know that you are such a big boy." "Tell my mom!" That's what I mean. We get affected by little things.

When you are settled, no matter how much garbage people are throwing on you, don't get affected by it. The person who does not get affected by it already shows they are not a weak person.

Spiritual people are very strong, brave. Only brave people can take that kind of trash, garbage, being called bad names, and criticism. The brave can do it. Weak people, their body will begin to shake. They get so affected by words or things mentally that their body becomes so shaky. They lose their temper, and they sometimes lose their own breath.

I can share with you that if the body and mind work well, the speech will be under their control too. They will not use bad language, and they will not use bad words towards others because they know people can get affected by them.

Imagine someone saying hurtful words to you - it's like a process. When you're called a bad word, it affects you and can make you angry. Even when someone shows a bad attitude, it stirs up anger, messing with your thoughts and causing chaos. You've likely experienced this. But then, think about a time when you're full of love. Like when you're fond of a little puppy and someone is yelling nearby - it doesn't bother you. The chaos within you disappears. Anger and negativity create chaos, while love is positive. When this positive feeling settles in you, it brings clarity and understanding to the surface. This clarity shields your mind from being affected, marking a shift towards being calm.

Psychologically, our thoughts flow from the inside outwards. From inner to outer. When thoughts flow from outside to inside it becomes two different things. Inside to outside or outside to inside. If your mind is already chaotic, and something from the outside is coming in that is chaotic, it will create even more chaos inside of you. The outer chaos will disturb your peace. When you do the opposite, and you go from inner to outer, then you are more settled and at peace. What will go outside reflects your inner state.

That's what people need to learn. You have to flow from inside to outside, not outside to inside. Society affects you because the chaos of the outside is entering you, and your inner being is not settled yet. When your inner being is not settled, you will be affected. When your inner being is settled, no matter if somebody throws stones on you, you will not be in a chaotic state. You're not going to get affected. And those people are the great people who remain the same in prosperity or in adversity. I call them great people. I don't call them enlightened, but I call them great people. At least their inner being is settled and not affected by things anymore. No matter whether they're in adversity or they are in prosperity. Both ways, they are the same. They learn by experience. Until experience happens in their life, they won't learn.

In some ways, if they don't ever go through that chaotic state, they're not going to settle because they will not have learned. If we are wise enough, we can learn from it. But if we are not wise enough, we will not learn from it. It is better, when the chaotic state is happening inside of you; you learn with it, be watchful, give a little time, or go through two or four hours. Eventually, it is going to settle down. How long will it go on for? It will click to you, "Hey, I am useless, I've wasted my whole time without meaning." Chaos is still there. So you have to settle down. The settling leads to the stillness of our being.

That's why it is better to work from the inside out. You're never going to be in a chaotic state. My advice for those who are already down, depressed, or anxious or they're in a weakened state, and then more chaos enters and becomes unbearable is to find a way to cheer yourself up. Be inspired. Find friends to uplift you. You have to change your situation. Take charge of your life. Remember, your nature is stillness.

The spiritual path is all about the inner work by yourself. Other people in society, or nature, will not change you to make you happy and to meet your expectations. They will always be who they are in society. They will have their moods; they will have their negativities; they will have their positivities. But it's up to you as an individual to not to be affected. It's your responsibility. You cannot blame other people for what's inside of you. We are taught in society to blame. We are taught that way.
It is not us; it is society.

And people think that society is very civilized. If it's a civilized society, then why are people getting affected so much? Civilized people are not supposed to affect another person. It is the so-called civilized society, which affects us a lot. It's an illusion. If somebody doesn't pick up a spoon a certain way or speak a certain way that they expect, with manners and politeness, they look down on the person or get affected by them.

The more rules that are in society, the more the rules will make a person stiff. There is no looseness in it. Let the person be loose, free, not stiff. Stiff people get affected very quickly. I don't teach people to be stiff. I teach people to be relaxed, to be always in stillness.

Stiffness will lead you toward religion and society; looseness and relaxation will lead you toward spirituality.

Chapter 18 —

Pushing through Life's Storms

We all want to follow the flow, that's the ideal, right? To have ease and flow carry us along our path. But, unfortunately, life sometimes gives us storms, and we have to face challenges that affect us emotionally or mentally, and we can become overwhelmed. People say, "I feel like everything is happening all at once." And the storm becomes so loud in our ears it's too much to handle.

During times like this, many people turn to their faith or religion to give them strength to get through the storm. But how should spiritual seekers navigate through life's storms? Human life is full of battles, full of chaos. This storm can impact our mental health, emotions, and sense of who we are. Life can be like a roller coaster of emotional highs and lows. We tend to think that all of these emotions are good, but I think emotions keep you in a cycle of suffering and pain. Of course, a few emotions, like love and compassion, might not bring storms into your life. Not the love that people are thinking about, I am talking about emotional love. Emotional love causes problems in people's lives. Why? Because they're not settled, they feel unsatisfied or restless. These feelings stir inside of them. How much easier life could be if we focused more on reality than on the fantasies in our minds?

People often focus more on their fantasies, which is why the storms, the chaos, won't go away. Imagining fantasies will keep you stuck in a cycle that's hard to come out of. Instead of fantasy, why not focus on reality? People will fantasize about finding their soulmate, the perfect man or woman. They fantasize about their dream job, living in a mansion, or becoming famous. They will spend their whole life waiting for their fantasy to arrive. But it is not a reality. They fantasize because they are acting and acting is not real. We have to come to reality, and reality is far away from emotions. Reality is far away from fantasies. Fantasizing will distract you, but the best thing you can do to calm down the storm, whether it's emotional, mental, or physical, is to check your desires. The soul is desireless. The soul doesn't entertain fantasies. The soul is beyond imagination. It is the mind that craves; it is the mind that desires, and where the invention plays. The mind begins to think, "Oh they have a big retreat, I wish I could have that." But then they don't want to work hard. The mind creates envy or jealousy, or greed. The mind creates fantasies. Is it good to have dreams? Yes, dreams are good as long as there is the right action to back them up. Come back down to reality. Come back down to Earth. That is my invitation to you. Reality doesn't come through fantasies. No. It can come through manifestation, though.

When people hear the word manifestation, they think of New

Age ideas, like the law of attraction. Manifestation is not a miracle. Manifestation is real, but for manifestation to work, you must first believe in your mind about what you want to be. You have to think deeply about what you believe yourself to be. If you can think of something, that is the universal law, whatever you think you will become. First, you have to start thinking, that is the first step. You are only focused if you think in a certain way. You must be focused to go forward. Being focused is also a challenging thing to do. To be focused, allow your thoughts to flow in one direction. If your thoughts are scattered too much, if they're not flowing in one direction, you can't focus.

In order to achieve focus, there are two steps to know. The first step is to learn how to concentrate. If you don't know how to concentrate, you cannot flow your thoughts in one direction. If your thoughts flow in one direction they have a lot of power. If they are scattered, they have no power. That's what fantasies are, they are scattered. However, fantasies can be focused too. If somebody's fantasizing and he or she puts all of themselves into it, then their thoughts go in the same direction. When they flow in one direction, then focus happens, and when focus happens, you come back to reality.

Manifestation cannot happen without focus. Once you are focused on what you want to be in life. Suppose a student goes into school, and he or she wants to get a Ph.D. in science or medicine, engineering, or philosophy. Whatever they think about, they can achieve but must remain focused. Otherwise, no focus, no degree, no diploma. Manifestation is not a new-age thing, but new-age people are in la la land. "Oh, we can manifest things!" First, you need to calm down your storm. Manifestation will never happen if your mind is going here and there, pulled in many directions. Manifestation occurs when a person is focused and you don't have to focus through your eyes. You can close your eyes and focus fully. Focus on one point. Maybe you will see in the dark light. That's why people are not doing the right thing. Doing the right thing creates a little spark in you. If you want to manifest, create a spark. And a spark will never be made if there is a storm.

Storms can bring lightning and thunder. You must calm the storm before it can ignite. Storms happen in darkness. That's why manifestation doesn't happen.

Manifestation happens when the darkness disappears. The dark will disappear if you know how to light the candle. How to light the bulb or how to light the candle? If there is light already, why do you have to light it? If you close your eyes, what happens? You see darkness, right? People go to the temple. They light candles there. I always tell people, "Light the candle or deepak where it is dark." But the temple is lit already, so they are going the wrong way. It is not a reality. That is fantasy, that is a new-age thing.

"Oh, God will create a miracle." "The universe will give it to me," or this god will create a miracle. That Shiva will create a miracle, or Jesus will create a miracle. Or Rama will create a miracle, right? But where are they lighting? Where there is no darkness. In the temple, there is no darkness; in the church, there is no darkness. So light the candle where there is darkness, and that darkness is in your heart. A little Arabic parable:

One evening there was a lady, named Rabia, and she was searching for something in the street, and children were playing. A child approached her and asked, "Mother, what are you searching for?"

Rabia replied, "Oh, my needle got lost."

"Your needle?"

"Oh, we have sharp eyes; we will help you."

There were ten children helping. They couldn't find it. And their eyes are very sharp to see it, this little thing.

They said, "Mother, we can't find it. Where did your needle get lost?"

To which Rabia said, "Oh, my needle got lost at my home."

The children were confused, "But why are you searching in the street?"

"My home is dark, but the street has light."

This parable has a lot of meaning. The needle represents soul. People search in the light because they are so fearful of the dark. Soul is hidden behind the dark, that is where you need to search.

People carry storms around with them in the form of their thoughts. The storm is the mind, and all of these thoughts are the dark rain clouds that distract you, they can scare you. Where there is a mind, there is no peace. It will always be a storm all the time. The mind loves its miseries and will not let you search for the real thing. You will not manifest anything because the mind loves to fantasize. The mind loves la la land, with endless thoughts and distractions if you let it.

Light a little candle, find the little spark, and as soon as you find the spark, you are going to manifest things. Manifestation is not far away from you, but it requires you to take the steps for concentration. You must flow your thoughts in one direction, and when thoughts flow in one direction, they have a lot of power. Like sun rays, they're scattered—trillions of rays. With a little magnifying glass, you can collect twenty rays, if they all flow in one direction, a fire is created. So that's what's going to happen.

When your thoughts flow in one direction, it creates a spark. The spark will light your heart, and once the candle of your heart is lit, the light will make manifestation possible. That's why we have to live in reality and love reality more than we love our fantasies. Then reality is a manifestation. Reality is when you find your needle in the darkness.

And where? Into the dark. How? Because you are scared to look into the dark. But that is how you'll find the spark in the dark. Learn how to walk into the dark. And once you learn how to walk into the dark, you will be surprised and see that something will be revealed to you. You will experience something. There is a place in the US where people teach "dark meditation." They have a retreat, a dark retreat, where they sit in a dark room and meditate. I would like to tell them, "Hey, you don't have to go into the dark. Just close your eyes."

But that's what la la land looks like. It is not a reality. Reality is learning how to walk into the dark without any anxiety, stress, disturbance, any scary thing, without any storm.

Thunderstorms happen all the time inside of us. So you must learn how to walk this path, like on the edge of a sword. That is the way manifestation is going to happen. Manifestation is a reality. Reality goes beyond fantasies. You must be in reality more than fantasies.

The real manifestation is the soul's work; even though the soul doesn't work, it's inspired by the soul. And to get to the soul, you must go beyond the storms. You have to go beyond your desires. You have to go beyond the fantasies. Most importantly, you must have a strong focus and great access to your concentration power. This might help you receive a vision, to get ideas on what to do and what to implement. The next most important step is to work hard because if you just focus and see something or realize something, it takes work to get there. To implement any vision, you have to work hard.

I'll give you an example of this. I envisioned Siddhayatan Tirth many years ago before moving to our what is now ashram in Windom, Texas. I envisioned Siddhayatan Tirth as a pilgrimage site. I knew that one day, thousands of people would come here to awaken their souls. Fifteen years ago, there was nothing here, just fields and cow pastures. I knew Siddhayatan would become a reality, and it wouldn't happen overnight. After 15 years now, we have the Tirtha, the meditation hills, the lake, the Tirthankara temple, and other statues that represent the qualities that we have within ourselves. There is still more to come, but full vision has not come to life yet, but it is still in the process.

My point is that you have to have the concentration to have the vision and then put in the hard work to make the vision possible. So manifestation is not like a miracle. Manifestation is the result of focus, vision, and hard work.

Not only do you have to remove the storms in your life, but also you have to make it happen on every level. So pour in energy physically, mentally, and emotionally to make it happen. Without *purusharth*, efforts, and hard work, manifestation can never happen.

All things are possible if you are ready never to give up. Siddhayatan Tirth is an example of even when the challenges come, even when negative people come, and even when people criticize or praise, you still keep going forward. It doesn't matter. You do the work your soul needs to do.

Chapter 19 —

Family Backlash after Awakening

Spiritual people may encounter resistance from their families when they begin their path or make changes.

When their family or close friends resist their new way of being, it complicates the spiritual person's life. This resistance might even cause anger to rise up. For example, let's say a family member says, "Oh, I thought you were learning about peace. Why are you yelling at me? I thought you were supposed to be peaceful."

If somebody is studying to improve, they don't want to be angry. However, when they do get angry, because they're human, their family can throw it in their face. They might say, "How can you get angry with us when you're supposed to be peaceful? I thought you said you're spiritual now. You don't seem like it." They mock you and try to press your buttons.

This type of situation is familiar. It's happened with many students who have adopted the spiritual path. In this chapter, I will share my advice for spiritual practitioners and students who face difficulties dealing with their families and friends who resist their new chosen path.

I remind students that the spiritual path is not easy. There are no stepping stones to follow. You must flow with all of life. Often families have their conditioning, expectations, and a certain set of rules and their place in society. So when a person chooses a spiritual path and starts to change from all those things, it can upset and confuse the rest of the family. For example, he or she wants to become a vegetarian or vegan, and the family doesn't like it because they are used to eating all kinds of meat. Now, that person doesn't fit in with the family, and every mealtime becomes an opening for an argument.

When people adopt the spiritual path, those closest to them sometimes cannot tolerate their transformation. It's kind of a jealousy because now that spiritual person is a mirror reflecting who the rest of the family are.

Let me tell you one very important thing. One king was in the forest hunting with his bodyguard, minister, and the head of the police. They were all protecting him while he hunted. Suddenly, the king got very thirsty, but they couldn't find any water in the forest. Then they saw one little hut with a pitcher full of water.

The king said to the policeman, "Why don't you go there and bring the water for me?" The police went to the hut, which a blind man owned. He said, "Hey you, blind man, give the water to us!" The blind man responded, "No, I'm not going to give you water. I know you are a policeman." He told the policeman to go away, so the police left without getting water for the king.

The king was still thirsty, so he sent the chief to bring him some water. So the chief approached the blind man's hut and called out, "Blind man, how much money do you want for the one glass of water?"

He said, "I'm not going to give you water. I know you are the chief of the police. I will not give you water. Go away from my hut."

The police chief left without water.

The king was still so thirsty, so the king went to the hut alone. And he said, "Sir, I am very thirsty. I would appreciate it if you can please give me one glass of water."

The blind man replied to the king, "Oh, please come and sit. I will give you some water. You can sit. Plus, if you need any other help, I am here to help you."

This friendly response made the king very happy. The blind man gave him water, and when the king finished drinking the cool water, he said, "Thank you, I don't need any other help."

The king continued, "Can I tell you one thing? You know how to respect kings."

"Well, you are like a king," said the blind man.

The king said, "Since you are blind, how did you know that the first person that came here was a policeman?"

"I knew him by his words and the way he ordered me. I knew that he was a police officer."

"But how do you know that second man who came here was the chief of the police?"

He said, "I knew he was the chief because he tried to bribe me with money."

The blind man continued, "Now, I'm going to tell you that every person, every human, is hidden behind their tongue and speech. You can find out who someone is by how they talk to you. I knew the way he ordered me that he's the police. I knew how he tried to buy me that he was the chief of police."

All human beings they're hiding behind their speech, their words, and their tongue. That's the way you will know them, who they are. And the blind man was right. As soon as somebody is transformed and adopts a better path, the family cannot tolerate it. Their authentic self comes out.

Because that person now who is transforming is causing that. Before that, they were delighted. They were happy. If somebody is drinking wine with them, eating meat with them, going here and there, traveling, staying in the hotel, enjoying, being entertained and happy. As soon as somebody begins to transform, the other person's ego is bound to react and, at first, get hurt. That is their authentic self coming out. They don't care whether it is their daughter, son, or whoever has adopted the spiritual path.

When a spiritual person looks pretty peaceful, happy, and

healthy, some people cannot tolerate when good stuff happens to them. They might adopt that system little by little, but those are rare families. Anyone who embraces a spiritual path can expect their family to react to some degree. Because before, they were like them; this person is elevating their life by growing. Other people cannot tolerate how the spiritual person is going higher than they are. Again, this is why their ego gets hurt. Behind the jealousy is the ego. While spiritual people feel happy and peaceful about their life, the family feels the way they live is not good enough anymore.

If the spiritual person doesn't react, no matter what the family says, the family gets even more triggered. They are seeking a reaction. Don't respond; that's it. That's what I tell people, I share how it is *they* who adopted the path of changing their habits, changing their thoughts, changing their eating. They want to be loving, kind, and merciful towards animals and all things, right? If they don't want to kill or harm animals by eating them, they think of the animals as a part of their family. So if they treat animals and the whole universe as a part of their family, shouldn't they treat their own family with the same respect and compassion? Therefore, even if someone is negative about their transformation, they should not react. That's what a family is like.

Spiritual people are like the white cloud. They don't react. White clouds don't resist. No matter if the wind blows to the west, it moves to the east automatically. If the wind blows to the north, it moves to the south quickly. No reaction. That's why spiritual people are just floating like a white cloud, and family and friends cannot tolerate that.

They will wonder why the spiritual person is just floating. Now they are enjoying real life. Babies float when they are in the womb. Nobody reacts toward the baby. The baby is floating and enjoying. That is the best time, the meditative state in the womb.

Do you know what some Hindus and Jains believe? They believe that the womb is the worst place to be. They think, "Oh, all this urine is going all over it." They don't understand that it is the baby's protection. They've made devotional song lyrics stating that "When the time comes that I never go to the womb again and again and again, that is the dirtiest place." They don't understand that it is floating and how the baby is the most spiritual being in the whole world. Being in the womb is the ultimate meditative state. They're like a white cloud. A white cloud doesn't have roots. If it is rooted, it cannot float. The baby is not rooted yet. It is floating. However, other clouds, like black clouds, fight. They're loud with thunder.

That's why I suggest to people that even though white clouds don't have rain. They have nothing to give, but they look beautiful in the sky. No purpose to being in the sky, but they look beautiful. So that's what it is. When somebody's transformed, the family, friends, and other colleagues, they will not like the person. And the person has to be prepared for that.

The path is for you, don't expect the path to be for them. Obstacles will be on your way and you need to be brave and strong to face it.

Some have the energy and full intention to be on the path, but the obstacles and the resistance from others can make them fail. Some have a very strong attitude, "If my family leaves me, I'm ok with that." Spirituality is not the weapon of the weak. It is for the brave.

In the beginning there will be conflict. In a way, it is to be expected. It's not supposed to be easy. People will go through hell in the beginning, at the same time, the real you comes to the surface revealing your strength.

If conflict arises, I suggest it is better to be quiet, peaceful and go higher. Don't expect anyone to understand or support you. Time can heal things. If you force them to accept you, it will create only more fight and trouble for everyone. Take the higher road and flow with it.

You might wonder about the karma collected because it seems like your decision to be spiritual is causing violence, pain and harm. It appears your parents are suffering because you are going on a different journey from what they wish for you. They'll say they are hurt by you. There is no karma collected because you are growing. Your intention is to grow. If you give up on your path, because of your own weaknesses, then your karma will begin to grow and you will suffer. Never give up. When you adopt the path of non-violence, it will lead you towards your freedom.

The biggest test for the spiritual person is the family. The family knows your buttons and triggers. Their words of criticism can be sharp. But if you keep moving on and walking forward on your path, that is the best for your soul.

Chaos will arise, whether you wish to be a monk or not, because the family will try to stop you. This is the test of the path. If you fail with your family, then you will not have much strength for the challenges to come on the path. How you deal with your family - emotionally and mentally - says a lot. I always teach: No matter how many obstacles, no matter how many difficulties that come on the way, be brave and move towards your victory. Spirituality is not an escape - it's learning to live in the world but not have the world live inside of you. Facing family, facing society is difficult, but thousands or more have gone before you and have succeeded. It is possible.

Once the journey begins in the right direction with right strength, right discipline, and right energy, it will become everlasting peace.

Chapter 20 —

The Beginning of Your Renewed Spiritual Journey

Every day, hundreds of thousands of people are discovering spirituality. Their curiosity may be sparked through attending yoga classes, learning about meditation, or taking a class on chakras. Whatever kind of introduction they have had, now they want to be on the spiritual path.

So how does a person have everlasting spirituality, so that it's always with them and never fades?

Meditation plays an important role in the spiritual journey - it is the path to enter the soul state. It's not an easy experience. I'm talking about real meditation. The superficial meditation that we hear a lot about these days is mainly calming down the mind to have a little bit of peace. It's a start, but for the spiritual practitioner, they're seeking to know who they are so one must put efforts to create the possibility of meditation to happen. You cannot expect to meditate. As soon as you try, it slips away from you. There are many areas of your life that you need to change and understand.

As I've mentioned before you need to have a healthy body, be able to create and sustain a lot of energy, know how to focus and much more. One of the biggest distractions to meditation is desire. Desire of anything will take attention away from your soul. That's why you need to understand your desires, and desires are limitless like the sky, once you get into your desire you're away from your soul. Soul has no desires. One of the hardest things to bypass is physical desire and that's why Brahmacharya needs to be understood more.

I shared before that Brahmacharya translates to celibacy unfortunately, but what it really means is "Being close to God." That there are no desires because you are always with God. What often happens is that people suppress their desires instead of understanding them. Suppression, or controlling it, will create hell inside of you. It's a resistance and because there is resistance the mind will never be settled. How to go deep into meditations when your desires, sexually or any kind, control you. You cannot control them. You can learn to understand, bypass and dissolve them. The best thing, as Tirthankar Mahavira taught, is to be aware. Awareness helps to reduce desires and as you become stronger, the less you'll be into your desires. Desires lead to suffering, in some way. Learn how to be desireless.

When awareness happens, thoughts disappear. A lot of people struggle with this. They want to control their desires or mind, but they get caught up in their thoughts. If they learned to be more aware, then I consider them spiritual.

The desire to take drugs, smoke marijuana, take ayahuasca, do mushrooms, that's all the desire of the mind. It's an excuse, in the name of spirituality, meditation or relaxation, or healing to fulfill a desire. Soul doesn't need those things. Soul requires a strong and healthy body, not a polluted one. It's a polluted experience and untrue. People fight and resist this truth. Why? Because deep down they are dependent and desire/crave it. They don't want to change. They want false experiences. For everlasting spirituality, one must go beyond these things.

Jiddu Krishnamurti suggested that there is an observer and the observed and ultimately both must be dissolved to experience meditation. If a person is observing an object, then there is a duality. Duality is an illusion. Nothing is separate from you. When you realize this kind of oneness and connection, meditation happens. If you're under the influence, this true oneness cannot happen, you're using something else to supposedly help you enter that state. It means the soul is dependent on marijuana, ayahuasca, mushrooms and LSD? Is the soul that weak it needs something? There is a big misunderstanding and it traps so many people. The ones who seek everlasting spirituality will start making steps to drop those things.

Spirituality becomes everlasting when observer and observed, subject and object, both disappear. When the observer disappears and the object disappears, meditation automatically happens. When this happens, spirituality begins.

I'm currently sharing with my students my interpretation of Patanjali Yoga Sutras, and also amending/correcting it where he might have gotten something wrong or it is mistranslated and misunderstood. There was a Jain Acharya who share a similar sentiment: "Vathu sahavo dhammo." The nature of the thing, is its own truth (dharma). So essentially, your true nature is your truth or path. How to find your nature is an interesting question and quest. Who are you? What is your nature? What appeals to you? What can no one take away from you because it is deeply a part of you? Whatever that is, that is your path.

Some people love animals, and animals help them to be spiritual. Some are parents, and children and the love experienced helps them get on the path and expand their love from their own children to all humans. Different things bring people to their own trance or experience of the soul. Some "lose themselves" and find total fulfillment in helping other people. Through this nature, spirituality is there. They can go deep into themselves.

There's a story I share sometimes about the scorpion and monk.

A monk noticed that there was a scorpion drowning in the river and so the monk went to the scorpion to save it. As soon as the monk tried to help the scorpion, the scorpion stung him. So the monk dropped him. He tried saving the scorpion 3 times until he was successful. A little boy who was observing them asked the monk, "If the scorpion was stinging you, why did you try to keep helping it?" The monk replied, "I cannot expect a scorpion to change his nature even if I'm trying to save him. The scorpion's nature is to sting and I cannot stop that. My nature is to help, and that's why I didn't give up."

Your nature is who you are and that is your path. Some people like different things - yoga, chakras, mantras, devotional hymns, running, singing - so many things out there. There are as many paths as there are as many souls. The thing is, most people feel they need to conform to a path that doesn't fit their nature. Spiritual guidelines are necessary on the path, but using one's nature is the best thing because spirituality can be experienced through it.

The time will come that once you really know your nature and discover what really appeals to you, you can one day go deep into your nature and enter a meditative state. Something will spark inside of you.

So-called spiritual people, these days, are mostly on the surface. As I mentioned in the very beginning, there are many masters in this universe but the real students are lacking. When you seek spirituality for the wrong reasons, you won't grow much, but when you seek it for the right reasons, though difficult, you will begin to blossom, transform, and the experience will be real.

Enlightenment is achieved when you approach the path the right way. There are so many distractions, can you master them? Every distraction or desire that you have will stop you.

In the Digambar sect of Jainism, there are naked monks. They believe that one must be male and naked to achieve enlightenment. It's very orthodox thinking and is a misbelief; however, if they wear one cloth, or a string touches them, then they think "Oh, we have a possession, we have a piece of cloth." A blanket, a cloth will stop their enlightenment? A cloth is stronger than their soul? It shows a lack of understanding. That is the difficult part with religion. The enlightened masters don't teach religion, they teach spirituality. Out of fear, religious people hold on to rituals and rules in hopes to preserve the teachings and follow exactly what their teacher did. Mahavira used to be naked, but he didn't say you have to be. But they miss these things, because they lack understanding. Being religious can be dangerous for the spiritual path in some ways. It's forced, fear-based, and unnatural. According to Jain text, Mahavira was carrying a divine blanket, *dev dooshya*, given by Indra, and one day it slipped from his body and he didn't care about it. So he became naked, naturally, not by force. Digambar monks force themselves to be naked. They're missing the point.

Spirituality is not forced. It's what comes natural to you. Same thing with being a spiritual student and doing practices. Discipline is good, but forcing things or an experience is unhealthy. The question is, what appeals to you? What is your nature? Because that path will lead you to everlasting spirituality.

When you start your journey from there, it is something, it is something concrete. If it is on the surface only, whatever you hear all the time, it is like you will suppress it. The mind cannot be controlled no matter what you do.

I think that's why a lot of people leave Catholicism in some way because they're searching for something more, but then they get stuck because Catholicism, or any religion, is a bunch of rules, and people are tired of rules. They're looking for flow but fall in the same ditch when looking for freedom.

Then in spirituality, they carry the same habits and ideologies but use spiritual language. But they still feel the same. They fall in the same ditch again and again and again. So they are moving, circling, getting distracted too much, and just falling off. Because their path didn't start for the right reason. What's the wrong reason? They wanted peace of mind. Hey, is there ever peace of mind? If you say mind and peace, they are east and west. That means it's the wrong reason.

If I will tell the truth, people will not like it, but that's what it is. Don't try to control your mind. You want to be enlightened? Don't suppress. Let go of control. Relax. Flow. Be. Find your nature. Understand and go beyond distractions and desires. Dissolve the observer and object. Be one with your soul.

An important aspect of everlasting spirituality is having the right guidance. Guidance is everything. If you can be on the path in a steady way, with someone who has succeeded and knows the pitfalls, it only makes sense to be under their training. They cannot save you, but they can guide you to be the best person you can be. They can point out your shortcomings so you can improve them. The words they share will click to your heart. You will experience your own glimpses of realization.

It doesn't mean that somebody has to teach you for that. It can happen by itself. It has happened with some people in the past. They didn't try to learn, but a click happened. And those people are more stable in their path. When a click occurs, there is a little glimpse of realization that happens. This click keeps them steady on the path because for a moment they "knew" something real, and so what they see in life is not real. They will follow the path more with a click. The spiritual path may begin without a click, usually from curiosity or second hand knowledge by reading a book. They get a little inspired. It makes sense logically, and then they still have to wait for the real click and realization to happen. Any book can inspire someone, even a novel, sometimes a spiritual book is just entertainment for the mind. When the real click happens, you will know it.

The spiritual path has to begin with the right reason. The right reason is something happened to you. When you have seen something, and realize something by yourself, nobody can take you away from that path.

As you progress, you get the real teachings, then you glow, then you shine, then you become bright, then your intelligence, your qualities, your everything increases.

You begin to blossom. That's what we need more of in today's society. People who are blossoming, transforming, and awakening. Total Transformation. It begins with a click. Everlasting spirituality begins with a click, a spark. Spirituality is the path of total freedom. When you have a guide, you won't go astray and it's like taking the freeway. It's up to you, but my deepest wish is for you to awaken your soul, realize by yourself, the truth and reality within.

Acharya Shree Yogeesh is a living enlightened master of this era and is the founder of the Siddhayatan Tirth and Spiritual Retreat, a unique 250+ acre spiritual pilgrimage site and meditation park in North America providing the perfect atmosphere for spiritual learning, community, and soul awakening to help truth seekers advance spiritually. Acharya Shree is also the founder of the Yogeesh Ashram near Los Angeles, California, Yogeesh Ashram International in New Delhi, India, the Acharya Yogeesh Primary & Higher Secondary children's school in Haryana, India, and his latest establishment, Siddhayatan Mandir Estonia, in Eastern Europe.

As an inspiring revolutionary spiritual leader and in-demand speaker worldwide, for over fifty years Acharya Shree has dedicated his life to helping guide hundreds of thousands of people on their spiritual journeys of self-improvement and self-realization.

It is Acharya Shree's mission to spread the message of nonviolence, vegetarianism, oneness, and total transformation.

CONNECT WITH US

Acharya Shree Yogeesh

https://acharyashreeyogeesh.com

Siddhayatan Spiritual Retreat Center
https://siddhayatan.org

9985 E. Hwy 56
Windom, Texas 75492
info@siddhayatan.org
903.487.0717

Acharya Shree Yogeesh's YouTube Channels
https://youtube.com/acharyashreeyogeesh
https://youtube.com/siddhayatan

Acharya Shree Yogeesh's Facebook Page
https://facebook.com/AcharyaShreeYogeesh

Acharya Shree Yogeesh on Instagram
https://instagram.com/AcharyaShreeYogeesh

www.ingramcontent.com/pod-product-compliance
Lightning Source LLC
Chambersburg PA
CBHW020925090426
42736CB00010B/1045